Tan, Nati and I walked out of Tans Dream, our ice cream and coffee shop on Ko Yao Noi. I kicked our Honda Wave into life and immediately started gasping wildly. Nati and Tan got on the back and Tan asked if I was OK, I said 'yes' but with some doubt. I had been having some odd symptoms recently and had had a check up at the hospital the day before, all was OK. I continued gasping wildly the few Ks towards our house, I called in for some gas, a very bad idea! I kicked the bike over again and things got much worse, I asked Tan to take over after 100m, I could barely stand while we did the swap. Tan drove the 400 or so meters home, I suddenly just had to go to the loo! Tan had to help me the 10 steps to the bathroom and I was completely ruined when we got there. When I was done   me to the bed and I collapsed on my back in a sphere of golden light, I was done, there was nothing left. I knew I would die in a few seconds if I couldn't get more upright, the room was getting dark outside the golden pool and I could vaguely hear Tan sorting the pillows I so needed. I looked down at me and said 'come on Steve' then I felt Tans strong hands pulling me up towards the pillows and get me a bit more upright. I was still gasping uncontrollably but I knew I would live for a while longer. I also knew there had been 3 people in the room.

The problem had been caused by an old overuse injury behind my right knee which had healed up during my 9 week fast. I wrote this book in 2 weeks, often doing 10-12 hour stints, I had allowed the old injury to rub against the edge of the settee I was sitting on, reopening the wound. This created a bleed, then a thumb sized clot which migrated to my lungs and settled near my heart. Oh, the exquisite irony! I had written a book describing just a very few of my only just survived adventures only to be almost killed by my settee! Never a Dull Moment eh?

Ching ching, my favourite Thai expression translates as 'really' !?

Many people reading this will only know my name because I happen to be Hazels Dad, many people reading this will think it will be all about climbing, its true, I have done a lot of climbing but I think of myself as a teacher. I spent about 30 years working with the most damaged, disabled and abused children in the country. I did a lot of guiding too, just another kind of teaching.

Life began properly for me when the family, Mum, Dad and my 2 younger brothers, Nick and John moved to Russets, Chewton Keynsham, an old stone built house in a huge garden surrounded by fields and woods. The lazy river Chew meandered slowly through the valley just 10 minutes walk away. It was paradise, and still is. The best present I ever got was an air rifle, the fields and woods were teaming with rabbits, pigeons and pheasants, the Chew was teaming with fish. Like most places in the World there is less now than there was then, except humans of course. I soon made friends with a like minded lad down the road, Richard, and soon after Cobber turned up. A Golden Labrador utterly untroubled by intellect, he came from a family that couldn't cope with him, every time they opened the door he would tear around the town trying to lick everyone, he was completely untrainable. All our time was spent roaming the valley with fishing rods and rifles, we knew every inch of every bit of woodland and river and could feed ourselves easily. If we couldn't shoot something we could always catch an eel. Everything was cooked Aboriginal style, cooking time depended on how hungry we were, mostly everything was burnt black on the outside and red raw on the inside.

Mum was a great Mum, Dad was a brilliant artist and Geologist but not quite so brilliant in the good Dad department. He wanted me to go to some horrible school in Bristol, it looked like a medieval prison. I signed my name at the top of the entrance exam paper then sat and twiddled my thumbs for an hour. He was not amused! It was very different a few months later when I came home with a brochure for Brymore, an agricultural school about an hour South, still in Somerset. I think I got 87% in that exam. I think Brymore is unique in that it has a farm attached, run by the boys with only a farm manager overseeing things. Every aspect of farming was covered with boys taking turns at running different departments. Pretty much all the boys lived in farming communities and even at the age of 13 were experts in many disciplines. Somerset is dairy country so most of the boys knew that side of things, not pigs or sheep for example. I worked on local dairy farms, up at 4am to milk 100 Friesians, home for breakfast then bail hauling till 6pm in the hay and straw seasons. Very hard work for not a lot! One 6 week summer holiday I worked pretty much every day bail hauling, in those days it meant picking up 20 + kilo bales and throwing them up onto a 3 meter stack on a trailer. The day I had to return to school Tony Warren turned up and gave me 10 quid, Mum took my 5 quid allowance off me, so I worked the whole Summer for sod all! I got very strong though. I got my first taste of climbing with John Floodpage, the farm manager, he took me and another lad to the nearest crag, I'm fairly sure it was Brean, all I remember is dodging falling rocks all day! Years later when I was climbing well Brean was still a testing experience with loose rock, rubbish gear and long runouts. The belay was usually 1 foot rammed down a rabbit hole on a loose 60 degree mud slope.

Brymore was a boys school. When I left at 16 having scraped a disappointing (for the old man) 4 'O' levels I went to Radstock Technical college to try and scrape a few more, but there were girls! Julie was my first girlfriend and I her first boyfriend, you can guess what we spent most of our time doing. Julie was a fun little pixie, Anne, tall dark and elegant, then Jill, a blonde, blue eyed angel. Jill and I spent quite a while together. When I left Radstock, I for some bizarre reason got a job in a jewelers shop in Bristol. I have absolutely no idea why! I spent most of my time walking up and down the nylon carpet building up a massive static charge to ensure the pestomers had a memorable experience. After about a year the area manager came to see me, 'Steve, the company has a great honour for you, we want you to come to HQ in Birmingham and train to be our youngest manager. 'Thank you' I said 'but actually I'm going to Cornwall to be a dustbin man'. 'Damn'! he said, 'I just knew you would say something like that'.

That Summer working in Cornwall changed my life. The family had been camping at Trewan Hall for many Summer holidays. It was a huge site on the grounds of an old stately house but we were always given a quiet corner in an old apple orchard with the company of the Tielemiers, a German family who always spent the Summer there. Christiana, the gorgeous daughter was the noisiest girl I have ever met! My job was to do everything that needed doing, collecting garbage and incinerating it, helping at the pool etc. There was a constant supply of girls of course. I shared a house with 2 others, Carol and Dave, they were both academics, not a species I had encountered before really. Dave once referred to an apple tree as a 'fructiferous arboreal manifestation', I was impressed! They asked me what my ambitions were, I had never given it a moments thought. Eventually they persuaded me to train to be a teacher. Carol was gorgeous! A small smiley little thing with a mass of curly black hair. We became lovers much to our surprise! Her second name was Duffy, I would like to think she is the same Carol Anne Duffy, the famous English poet. It wouldn't surprise me at all!

I spent the next year working on a building site before going to Teacher Training College, it was hilarious! The boss was a racist old bastard by the name of Ken Baldwin, there was an ancient paddy bricky called George and a great lad the same age as me by the name of Henry Coggins. Henry and I were always competing to see who could carry or lift the most. We would climb ladders with 150 kg of cement on our shoulders or push a wheelbarrow piled impossibly high with concrete blocks. Lunch hour was spent in the pub, 3 pints of Bass and a pork pie. We got very strong!

The old man didn't think much of my chances of getting into college, Mum said 'go for it Darling'. The interview was meant to be 20 minutes of talking about who knows what? I spent a great hour and a half discussing long range pike tactics. He just said at the end 'your in'. Carp and Pike fishing was my passion in those days, I spent ridiculous amounts of time at beautiful lakes and rivers all over the SW with good mates, usually not catching anything. We referred to our obsession as 'ing', its like fishing but without the fish bit.

When I got started at college we had to do the 'sausage machine', students from previous years explained all the facilities, clubs and interest groups you could join. Beverly was one of the providers and had already decided from my photo that I belonged to her. Who was I to complain? She was gorgeous! I was still with Jill in Bristol, Bev was still with Dave in Devon, it worked! I had signed up for a science course but after a few days stewing in a classroom I swapped to PE, and my life changed again. Part of the PE course was outdoor education. The college was the proud owner of Gelli Iago, a lovely little house snuggled below Cnicht in Snowdonia. A bunch of us would go there weekends and walk, teaching ourselves mountain skills and navigation using map and compass, I loved it. Rain, shine, snow or clag we went out every day possible. One day in Winter I went out with 2 mates Paul and Phil hell bent on climbing a snow face in Cwm Idwall, we had one ice axe and one 50 meter hawser laid rope between us. I ran out the whole rope then fell off resulting in a 100 meter fall, I landed on a rock on my ass and left blood stains everywhere for the rest of the day.

Every now and then I would see people climbing rock walls and this piqued my interest. One weekend in Bristol I went down to the Avon Gorge and loitered until a couple of climbers showed up. I told them I was interested in climbing and could I play with them? They tried a Hard Severe but couldn't do it, I could. Then for some strange reason we went to the Suspension Bridge Buttress to try the arete. At Hard Very Severe it was much harder! They couldn't do it so I had a go. Every now and then I would find a bit of metal and call down for advice on what to do about it. The guys had given me a rack but I had no clue what to do with it. I guess I did that 40 m pitch with 3 bits of gear. I was hooked! I had discovered the meaning of life. I joined the college climbing club and went to the Roaches, the nearest crag to college. One bit of rock interested me in particular so I set off up it, solo. Halfway up I got completely shut down. I couldn't go up down or sideways so eventually I jumped off into a Rhododendron bush. I looked it up in my guidebook, Death Knell, E45c, a good route for people who like jumping off into Rhododendron bushes. In Bristol I had started meeting some of the local climbers. Arni Strapcans took me under his wing and we went to Stanage one weekend. He pointed me at Right Unconquerable, no worries! I can climb HVS, I set off and was pumped stupid in about 20 seconds. Grit ain't the same as Avon! Arnis cruised and I followed, predictably pumping out halfway. 'I'm coming off Arnis'! 'its OK, Ive got you on a stitch plate', 'whats a stitch plate'? I wailed as I slumped onto the rope. Very sadly Arnis died soloing the Route Major on Mont Blanc. If he had not he would certainly have become a world class climber and mountaineer. He was the first of many, many friends to die over the years to follow, mostly in the mountains. I got good quick! There was a rubbish climbing wall at college. I got permission to scratch out tiny holds in the mortar between the bricks, I would spend hours soloing up and down the wall wearing big leather mountain boots. I spent all my time hitching around the UK, living on my measly grant. Just climb, climb, climb. I would return to college a few days before the end of term, plagiarize all the text books and scribble out a few essays. Amazingly I passed! E3 in a few months then an early ascent of Right Wall within a year, I was on fire! But not using chalk. Arnis was dead against chalk as were we all in the SW, Pat Littlejohn in particular. Pat for anyone who doesn't know is one of the Worlds great sea cliff, and beyond explorers. Until he capitulated of course! I never understood chalk. Here we go I hear you all cry, Findlay on his favorite topic again, BORING! Its filthy, its aid, it reduces friction, anyone can work that out. The best friction you will ever get out of a piece of rock is when you first touch it with nothing between it and you. So many climbers claim to be environmentalists, fucking hypocrites, you walk up to a bit of rock and assume you have the right to change it, you don't! You slap white powder on rock that's millions of years old and if its overhanging there it stays, for ever. I saw a sign in Northumberland once, written in large letters with chalk on a boulder. 'Take you're litter home'. Chalk is just litter justified by people who aren't good enough to climb without it. Chalk is all about ego. Think about it. I never thought of myself as a particularly good climber but apparently on siting 7c, on gear, without chalk is quite good. My daughter tells me I'm a dinosaur, ching ching?!

My last day at university was interesting! I was doing my last teaching practice in a particularly rough part of Birmingham, the best bit was Friday afternoons when I had to take the 6th form girls trampolining. Use your imagination! The head girl was stunning, very fond of star jumps and microscopic see through knickers. As I walked out of the school gates for the last time a car drew up with 2 guys inside, they were Father and Brother of a little shit I had chucked out of class a few days before me, 'oh fuck' thinks I. Dad reaches down and comes up with a length of metal pipe. I'm not fuckin avin this I thought and kicked the door shut as he was halfway out, really hard! I think I hurt him pretty bad. I turned round to see the school management team looking at me. 3 years down the drain methinks. The Head came over, shook my hand and said 'thank you Mr Findlay, we've been hoping someone would do something like that for a long time'.

I went climbing. I climbed and I climbed and I climbed. Everyday and all day. It didn't matter where or with whom. One very fun trip was to Tremadog, there I did Vector with Rowland Edwards, a N Wales legend, the second ascent of The Atomic Finger Flake, Banana's and Sultans of Swing with a very young Andy Pollitt. A long time after when Andy was writing his book 'Punk in the Gym' he reckoned he led the crux pitch, hmm, 'don't think so mate'. Andy always kept a record of his climbs, I led the crux pitch. Highly recommended if you haven't done it already. I also did Strawberries with 1 fall, I always lost interest if I couldn't flash a route.

My favorite place was the Verdon. I first went there with Arnis, Steve Monks and Neil Beggs. Arnis and Steve where au fai with bigger European stuff, Neil and I had never seen anything remotely like it. It was big! The route to start with was Luna Bong, Not hard, not long but a good route to get us all in the groove. Arnis and Steve set off early, Neil and I had sat up late drinking cheap local red wine and set off late. When we arrived at the top of the crag our mates had just pulled over the top. Beetroot red! They had been climbing in the sun all morning. Lesson no. 1. Neil and I rapped in, the poor lad was terrified and I didn't blame him, the exposure was something else. At nearly 60m down I had to swing in and pull on a twig to get to the belay. Neil followed, almost in tears, ab followed ab until we were on the ledge still only halfway down the wall. We had a nice cruisy afternoon in the the shade.

I fell seriously in love with the Verdon, the climate, the people, the 1 Frank / liter 'ving', the 1000 ft sheer walls of perfect limestone and the river, far, far below. I have no idea how many times I went to the Verdon but my best memory is of hitching down on my own, setting up my very simple camp and meeting Richard. He was with some other French guys who recognized me from the front cover of Crags, the climbing mag of the day, Richard needed a partner and invited me over to their camp for dinner. I explained that I had very little cash and couldn't return the favour. He lifted the boot of the car to reveal an enormous cache of food and booze the likes of which I had never seen before! Richard and I where well suited standard and experience wise, and we liked each other. We climbed and we climbed and we climbed. We weren't bothered about grades, it was mileage we were after. One day we did a route called Dingomaniac, easy for us. Richard led the top pitch which went straight up from the the belay, a fairly long traverse right then he disappeared round an arete, along with a lot of rope, then with a blood curdling scream he appeared level with me and 15 m out from the rock. He had got to the the top of the finishing gully, slipped on a bunch of dry leaves and went at least 40m! The next day we went to do Pichne Bull, one of the trickier routes at the time,11 pitches.

Richard went to lead the first easy pitch to calm the demons. He came back after 20m, 'Steve, my head, it is fucked'; Ching ching!? We still did it. After a couple of weeks we had run out of money, food and booze so Richard invited me back to his parents place in Grenoble. Turned out his Dad was Ambassador to Tunisia and they lived in a polished wood mansion overlooking the city. His sister was absolutely stunning!

Normality?

Work, it comes to all dirtbags eventually, I got a job for a while selling loft insulation. I had been a team leader for these guys before and made a lot of cash. They gave me a smart car and all sorts of allowances. I never sold a single square millimeter of insulation, I just went round houses and said 'the government wants to pay for you to have your loft insulated, every single person said ' no thanks'. Ching ching!? Somehow Angela and I had become presidents of various sites of the college, she was very hard working and diligent, I just went climbing. I have no idea why people kept voting for me, I didn't do very much and I was a terrible public speaker. I think it was because I could negotiate with the authorities. We got together at some point after college and fell in love. Angela moved in with me in a lovely leafy street in Bristol. She was teaching and I soon found some great work with Youth Opportunities, a government created organization to try to combat high youth unemployment rates. Some of my climbing mates worked there, Nipper Harrison, Steve Marriot and bunch of really great down to earth guys and girls. I went for an interview, John, the boss just said 'your a climber eh'? Yep, start next Monday'. 'OK'. We were working in Hartcliffe, a poor downtrodden estate to the South of Bristol, the kids were hilarious, many were damaged. Johnny Walters was my favorite, he would rub a mixture of toothpaste and margarine into his hair every morning and pull it up into massive spikes, this was all good till it rained. We were basically social workers but teaching the kids some life and work skills. They would get a pay check on a Friday and we would take them into town to pay into the bank. Probably the most important lesson we taught the kids was how to go to a boozer and not get into a fight.

I started climbing with Nipper, he was an ace climber then, one of the best. He was funny, smart, and ruthless. We were both into onsiting, no one understands that any more, wankers! Every weekend was in Pembroke, we would drive Friday evening after work, get hammered in the Bosherston pub then crash in the church doorway. The next day we went climbing, and I mean climbing, everything onsite, me no chalk. Nipper was brilliant at spotting new lines, it took me a while to learn that skill. We would climb till it was dark then get hammered in the pub, smoke some resin and do the same the next day. Sundays the old guy would come and open the church, if it was wet he would say 'dont bother lads', if dry, 'come on lads, get yourselves out'. To Mrs Westons of course! The Queen of Pembrokshire,

I worked in Hartcliffe for a couple of years until I felt a strong urge to go to Yosemite. My first ever flight was to Seattle, Yosemite the long way. The immigration officer asked if I had more than $15,000 on me, 'do I look like I have more than $15,000 on me'? 'just answer the questions sonny'. Welcome to America! I caught a bus outside the airport and offered the driver $10, he asked if I had change, I asked why he didn't have change. 'It ain't worth dying for sonny'. Welcome to America! I found a climbing shop and asked if anyone fancied going climbing, an Asian American lad said 'yes, come and stay at my place'. It turned out to be a house full of Greenpeace activists and I had a great time for a a week or so. Climbing in the Cascades, whale watching in Pujet Sound and Frisbee golf. When I decided to head for Yosemite the guys dropped me off on the road South. The first car stopped and the driver offered me a doobie. 'you get high man'? In the UK I used to do a little rather indifferent resin, this stuff was completely off the scale! When he dropped me off I felt fine, it was only when a cruiser pulled up and asked me why I was hitching in an illegal place did I find I couldn't speak. 1 cop searched me and found my British passport, 'fuck, imagine the paperwork' he said. They dropped me off in a legal place and as they pulled away the other guy goes 'next time someone offers you a smoke I should say no if I was you sonny'.The next big lift was with a guy in a beat up old truck with a chopped down Harley and 2 huge huskies on the back. As soon as I got in he asked where I was going, 'California', 'why you going there? its the weirdo capital of the World'! 'Where you from'? 'England'. 'Oh yeah, that's where you all sit around in castles drinking tea all day ain't it'? He was driving non stop from Anchorage to Pheonix (3,600 miles) fueled only by speed, chewing tobacco and coffee every 50 miles. I had never had American roadhouse coffee before and came out totally wired every time. We got on really well, he was interested in my climbing and he told me some great stories. He had spent 6 months panning gold in Alaska and made about $250,000, a lot in 1979! His mate had made twice that and was staying on for more. Apparently there are some old timers out there who have amassed huge fortunes and keep it hidden away, in logs and caves etc. They would think nothing of killing someone they suspected was out to rob them, nor the Mounties. They would go to Anchorage for 1 month each summer, take the top floor of the best hotel and spend enormous amounts of cash on girls, booze, drugs and steak. My friend took me hundreds of miles out of his way and dropped me right outside

Camp 4, even dismantling his 4 rifles to get into the park. Driving into Yosemite for the first time is mind boggling!

I soon bumped into Andy Parkin, a man I had not met before but I knew him of as one of the best climbers in the UK. He went on to become one of the truly great climbers, mountaineers and explorers. Ever! He is also a very talented artist. After watching me layback a jamb crack he said 'you better learn how to jamb youth, and pretty damn quick! Giant splitter cracks do not exist in the UK or the Verdon. I learned how to jamb pretty damn quick under Andy's guidance but its not a disciple I ever got particularly good at. He also taught me the fine art of living on nothing, scams in restaurants, free supermarkets and cheap Sunday breakfasts. The Ahwanee hotel did an incredible eat all you can breakfast for $5. 2 Norwegian lads were asked to leave one Sunday because in the view of the management they had eaten more than was humanly possible. A whole bunch of climbers from all over the World were drinking one night and someone thought it would be a good idea to break into the compound holding all the hire bikes, we wound the rangers up for hours, tearing around the valley, if they got too close we would just nip into the forest. 'Come out'! they shouted, 'fuck off'! we replied. Eventually they tired and we returned the bikes. I really got into slab climbing, the Apron had some particularly smooth and ice polished rock. In those days we were climbing in EB's, non sticky rubber and you really needed to rearrange your eyesight. I did quite a few no falls first ascents. I also met a great German lad, Wolfgang, we did the NW Face of Halfdome together. In those pre cam days we had a rack of hex's and some wires. About half way up, I was grovelling up a chimney and the gear loop on my Willans harness broke, all the hex's went clattering down the face, we rescued a few but did the rest of the climb with some big runouts. Because we had to wait for some slow lads in the morning we got to Big Sandy in the dark, I had to place a wire round a corner blind, if it had pulled I would have smashed into some boulders way below. A British mate, Andy March was on Big Sandy once. He and his mate where woken at dawn by a quiet humming sound, about 20 meters away was a flying saucer, they watched it for a few minutes then it zipped off at an incredible speed!

I had a bash at the Salathe Wall with one of my best mates, Steve Massey. Steve had led the Hollow Flakes pitch and I was jumaring down so I could swing into the flakes. The pin at the top ripped and I went flying down the wall head first with the haulsac attached to my harness. I knew I was going to die, such a long way! My CMIs stopped me, I reckon any other make would have exploded. I sent them to Wild Country to have them checked, they sent them back with a note telling me I was a 'lucky bastard'! Steve died a couple of years later, squished by rocks on the South Face of the Aguile Du Fou. I was very sad about that.

When I got back I returned to Youth Opportunity's but this time in Southmead, a large poor estate on the North side of Bristol. It was very similar to Hartcliffe but with a slightly darker feel. Many of the kids were into glue, undoubtedly the worst drug I have ever encountered. Kids would pour tins of glue into big plastic bags and get dangerously hammered. We had this dozey little Welshman for a manager and the girls just took him to pieces, they had no respect for him whatsoever. I pleaded with them to leave him be, but they just said 'he's a fucking wanker Steve', and they were right. Darren was a really smart lad and a great natural athlete but he would turn up some mornings in a glued up mess and I would have to tell him to go home. Many years later I was looking round a huge department store and there Darren was! In a security guards uniform no less. We just cracked up! 'Honest Steve, I'm head of security and all the other lads are working here', a whole crew of the worst petty thieves I have ever met! It was so cool to see those guys again.

We did some good jobs the couple of years I was there, the kids expressed themselves painting murals, we painting schools and built a large garden area for a disabled unit. Once we were building a playground and one of the lads hit a large pipe with his spade, the next day a guy in a suit turned up to see what we were doing. The pipe was part of the strategic fuel system, but how did they know we had touched it? Spooky!

We were asked to do a bit of building work at a small special school nearby, Highdene, Angela had worked there for a while and they soon offered me a job with more money and longer holidays. Highdene was an old house set in several acres of grounds, it catered for very damaged and abused boys mainly from London. For many it was the last chance before prison. I learned a lot at Highdene! My job title was science teacher, I never taught a single syllable of science the entire 7 years I was there. Social worker, confidant, friend, yes, teacher?, maybe. Terry and Bill ran the place and had an interesting philosophy, no rules. I ended up disagreeing with them quite strongly but most of the time it was great. The staff were very committed and ranged from salt of the Earth women with no qualification other than life experience to people like me with teaching degrees. I loved working with Rose Dunkerton, as down to Earth as it is possible to be, the kids loved and respected her because she loved and respected them. Most of the boys had seen precious little of either. We always had between 9 and 14 boys, below 9 we lost money, above 14 things got very difficult to manage. Most of the time it was calm and peaceful but if we got the wrong mix things could get out of hand very quickly, especially at night and often just after a full moon. I always did a night shift on a Monday, I worked from 2pm Monday till 4pm Tuesday, if it was quiet it was great if it wasn't, it wasn't. Some nights I sat up late with Pete the night man while the boys trashed the place, and I mean trashed! We never intervened, we just made sure no one got hurt. One time I watched Tommy Smith destroy a cooker with his fists. When he finally stopped I said 'nice one Tommy'. 'What do you mean' he asked? 'Its a cooker Tommy, not a person'. Tommy had been pushed from care home to care home his entire life. Usually things calmed down at 1 or 2 am and we would coax the boys upstairs. Most of them stayed up really late every night unable to sleep and not surface till midday. Sometimes in the early days I would get frustrated, Terry always had a few wise words, like 'Steve, there is no point in trying to understand the maladjusted mind', or, 'Steve, this work is liking trying to push water uphill, if you get 1 drop over the top, you've won'.

One day I went to see Terry, 'I want 3 months off to go to the Himalaya'. 'If I say no you will just go anyway wont you'? Yep.

The first time I went to the Himalaya was very nearly my last. A small group of us decided it would be a good idea to try a new route on the S side of Cho Oyu, a ridiculously big mountain on the border of Nepal and Tibet. Just before we went I had a day on the Grit with Al Rouse. 'What about bad weather Al'? He said 'there's no such thing as good weather or bad weather Steve, there's just weather' A good metaphor for life in general. Al very sadly died coming down from the summit of K2. Al was one of the all time great climbers and mountaineers.

Cho Oyu (Goddess of Turquoise)

I knew nothing about Asia, I knew nothing about Asians, I knew nothing about poverty on a vast scale and I had never had to walk round a dead man on a pavement before. Lydia Bradey and I went into Colcatta for a look see and had to leave after a few hours, it would take a couple of days to cope with what we where seeing. Next, Kathmandu, a lot nicer! We all got busy buying food, pots and pans and all sorts of stuff I had never even seen before. We were guided by our small and lovely Sherpa team all arranged by the splendid Bikrum Pandi. One afternoon I was looking out of the hotel window and couldn't help noticing a large open water tank with a whole flock of crows parading round the edge, hmm, methinks, that might not be so good. We had to change our sterling into small denomination Nepali Rupees. One evening a guy in a long coat and motor cycle helmet came to guide us. Harry, an ex Marines officer and I were nominated to go with him as we were the biggest guys. Our dodgy looking guide took us down a labyrinth of dark alleys to a scruffy little room where the money changer lived. We had 4000 quid, you could stick a zero and more on the back for the same trip nowadays. A medium sized wad of 20 quid notes converted into an entire suitcase full of local currency! After a few days we set off, a day on a bus led to the road head, then a 3 week walk. I was just constantly gob smacked! We were walking across the grain of the country, up huge hills, down huge hills, all through the most amazing country. Forests of Rhododendrons and giant Magnolias, carpets of Primula's and orchids in the trees that sparked off a lifetimes interest, passion and obsession. Gorgeous little villages full of gorgeous people and gorgeous little kids who would run up and shout Namaste! We would sleep in tents, but one night Matt thought it would be a good idea to sleep in one of the tea houses. It wasn't. He came down the next morning covered in flea and bed bug bites. We passed by Lukla then on to Namche Bazarre. I dont know how many times I've been to Namche but in 1984 it was a very different place to how it is now. We stayed in our Sirdars house, a classic Sherpa house, animals downstairs, human animals on the 2nd floor, feed and firewood on top. If you needed a shit in the night (I did a lot) you had to dodge cantankerous yaks so you could take a dump off the cliff at the end of the street. Now the same place is a posh hotel with sparkly tiled bathrooms. After Namche the landscape opens up and the full majesty of the region appears, Ama Dablam, Lhotse, a glimpse of Sagarmatha, after a few days I looked out of my tent one morning to see Cho Oyu, 'hey Pemba, we nearly there', 'yes Steve only 1 more week'. The enormity of the Himalaya still hadn't sunk in. I had been to the Alps a few times and been very impressed, but this was a whole different ball game. A few days more and we dropped down onto the Ngozumpa glacier, enormous of course, and set up base camp. We had sorted all our food and kit into boxes arranged so if we lost 1 box we wouldn't lose all of 'something'. I was chief scrounger for the trip and had scrounged a load of golden syrup, at some stage the lids had popped off and every single item was covered in super sticky syrup. The boys and girls who had portered for us stayed at BC for a goodbye party, I was very impressed when the party fizzled out and they all just got into a large pile and kept each other warm, it was pretty bloody cold, I guess they did the Penguin thing. The S face of Cho Oyu is of course huge, a Polish team had done an incredibly hard and dangerous looking line on the left of the face, we were looking to do something a little gentler way to the right, it was very long though! We began exploring, looking for a reasonable route, it was basically a glacier face, riven by countless crevasses but there was a snow ridge running down from Ngozumpa Ri, a pimple on the ridge that ran from Cho to Gyachung Kang, a very seldom climbed peak just a tad under 8000m. A couple of us went up with Jumbezi Pemba Lama to set up camp 1, our route took us up close to an icefall that was constantly crashing down huge chunks of ice, then into a couloir surrounded by seracs. It was blindingly hot! The thermometer maxed out at 212f, I could smell the nylon I was wearing. At one point Pemba dropped into the soft sludgy snow and announced it was time for an oxygen break, time for a fag. We stayed there a night, left our supplies then dropped back down to BC. I got out some Tabasco sauce and offered it to Pemba, he upended it, had a swig and pronounced 'that aint chilli sauce'! He found a nice flat rock, put a fist full of chilies, a fist full of garlic and a very generous pinch of salt on it. Then with a fist sized rock ground it into a pulp, a pressure cooked new potatoe dipped in Sherpa Korsani (life threatening chilli) is a thing of wonder! Entertainment at BC was easy, just sit back and watch the huge avalanches crash down just a K away, often we would have to hide from the clouds of ice dust that billowed down the glacier.

I was ill. I had got the shits in Kathmandu, I was coping with it but the higher we got the worse it got. By camp 2 I was in a bad way. The gruesome dried food just went straight through and I was losing a lot of weight. I decided to bail. The first day on the way down I broke through 2 crevasses, hanging from my rucksac and ice axe, inky depths below me and feet kicking in space. The second day I broke through an area of clear ice on the glacier, again suspended by my rucksac 10m above a raging river. I hauled myself out then stood looking spellbound at a Tortoiseshell butterfly sunk 1 inch down into the clear ice. I crawled down the glacier until the Sherpa's saw me, they basically carried me into BC and gave me a liter of dahl. Nipper and I had a quick conflab and decided it was not for us. We turned a 1 week walk in into a 2 day walk out to Lukla. I sold all my high altitude gear in Kathmandu and vowed never to return. Nipper and I decided it would be a good idea to post some Temple Balls (a particularly good resin) back to the UK, we wrapped it in plastic several times and popped it in the post box, we stood back a few meters and cracked up, we could smell it across the street! We did get some back in ice axe handles though. When I got home Angela took me to the Doctor, he took 1 look at me and phoned for a taxi to take me to Ham Green infectious diseases unit. I had lost nearly half my body weight. It took a long time to get strong again, a friend took me to Symonds Yat for my first attempt at climbing, he cruised the E1 5b, I reached for the first jug and nothing happened, I could not even get off the deck.

Back at Highdene a new lad turned up, Andrew Dixon. A really nice smart lad from the back streets of London, he had been looking after his younger brother and sister for quite a few months after Mum and Dad abandoned them. He fed them exclusively on fish and chips when he could steal some money. The morning he arrived I took him down the garden to meet the animals. We had an enormous pig by the name of Mabel, a few sheep, 4 goats and a gaggle of very noisy and aggressive geese. When Andrew saw the lambs he said 'wow ! I've never seen sheeps pups before'. One thing I never did was read other peoples views of the kids, I preferred to come to my own opinions. Andrew slotted in quickly. Some of the lads took ages, one poor lad wouldn't take his coat off for months and hoarded food under his bed. Rose worked hard with him! Andrew was a genius rapper, he would get up on a table and belt em out at any opportunity. I introduced him to fishing and we spent a lot of time together on lakes and rivers around Bristol and Somerset. I always got a hit from being paid to go fishing with Andrew. Many years later I paid a visit to Veals fishing tackle shop, somewhere I had been going since I was a kid. An old friend there said 'hey Steve, a lad called Andrew Dixon came in a while back and said if you ever see Steve Findlay tell him he saved my life'. Andrew was with his 3 year old daughter, he had married a solicitor and now lived in Cardiff. Quite often with these kids you don't know know if you got that drop of water over the top till the next generation and the cycle of abuse is broken.

Kangar Punsum 7500m

A similar crew that went to Cho Oyu decided it would be a good idea to try and climb the highest unclimbed mountain, Kangar Punsum in Bhutan. I went to see Terry and said I wanted 3 months off to go to the Himalaya, 'if I say no you will go anyway wont you'? Yep.

I had a very happy if hard and very cold time on Kangar Punsum. The walk in was gorgeous and we met nomadic yak herders that had never seen white folk before. I teamed up with Lydia and forged a way up to camp 1, I reckon I did one of, if not the, hardest and most dangerous pitch's I've ever led that day. A very long vertical snow pitch that was about 80% air, it was incredibly tenuous! 1 axe at arms length in the snow trying to get a tiny bit of purchase, feet slowly collapsing. I was only tied into an 8mm polypropylene fixing line, Lydia looked very small perched on her little boulder far, far below. Well over 6,000 meters. We eventually found more solid ground but couldn't find a good camp site. We hacked out a ledge on a 60 degree ice slope only just big enough for 2. We put up our experimental single skin Gortex tent, it was rubbish. Our breath just froze on the inside and showered back down on us. We took turns every hour to go out and clear the spindrift that was pushing us off. It was so cold my plastic watch hung up in the roof completely disintegrated. We dropped some gear off then headed back down to ABC, the next pair found a good camp a few hundred meters higher. The winds started picking up. The others (including Jeanette Harrison who died on Dhaulagiri, a very tough little lady) put in some very hard work pushing the route along the Dinosaur ridge, we had to clip in and literally haul the rope out of the sky, belays were shit and a long way apart. Eventually we got camp 2 sorted but the wind was insane! The jet stream was slamming into the top of the mountain not far above us and blasting plumes of snow thousands of meters higher. Lydia and I went out to check out a rock buttress which looked maybe OK, a massive area of cornice broke off just millimeters in front of our crampon points. Incredibly, we saw Black Neck Cranes migrating South directly over the peak, 8,000m easy. The way on ahead didn't look too bad but not in those conditions. Down down down. 4 of us ended up in the tent at C1, fully dressed and ready to go, sure enough, at dawn one of the best tents ever made just exploded! I would have had a very hard time getting down that day if Lydia hadn't done the knot changes for me. My hands were frozen solid and I lost all my toe nails. We couldn't walk out as there had been huge snowfall lower down. The Indian Army eventually found us in helicopters and flew us to Paro, 40 minutes to cover what had taken 2 weeks to walk. While I was on the mountain I had thought a lot about being a Dad, Ben was with us, Angela was keen on a second, I decided that this game was way too dangerous. I wanted to be around for my kids.

I went to Cho Oyu in 1984, Ben turned up in 1985, Bhutan was 1986. I guess I started at Highdene in 83, but after Bhutan I realized I was disagreeing with Terry's philosophy more and more. He was too generous with the boys, I felt they weren't learning the life skills they were going to need when care stopped at 19. These kids were vulnerable enough without being chucked out into a tough World badly prepared. The boys were driven into town instead of being shown how to use the buses for example. One night they wanted to go to an amusement arcade in town, something I strongly objected to, along with several other members of staff, but to keep the peace I capitulated. A mile down the road I just thought 'fuck it' and turned round. All hell broke loose. When we got back we had a massive row in the car park and one lad actually hit me. We had always got on well. A few hours later he came and apologized and said 'actually Steve, you are right'. Andre was the dude. A very smart strong black lad, I would be very surprised if he's not living in a mansion overlooking the Thames and driving a Porsche. Or he could be in prison of course. Nothing much changed though, Terry's 'allowances' kept increasing, I think he had been in the business too long and was getting tired. You cant use money to keep the peace. Terry and Bill asked me to take on the management of the school, I said I would if I could do it my way but they couldn't accept that. That was OK with me, I had done 7 years, done my bit, I was stressed, it was time to move on.

St Christophers and Charlie

John, the head of school showed me into the dining room at lunch time, about 30 people with hugely differing disabilities were sitting down to lunch. This was basically the interview, I could feel John watching me as we talked, I was struggling not to burst out laughing, it was the funniest thing I had ever seen! I had never had much to do with disabled folk previously so this was an education. Many needed to be fed, some were fine on their own and everything in between.

The school was based on Rudolph Steiner's philosophy, his quotes are very interesting and educational, one of my favorites is. 'Our highest endeavour must be to develop individuals who are able out of their own initiative to impart purpose & direction to their lives'.

I realised while doing my teacher training I had not learned anything about how to actually teach. The state system doesn't seem to have any philosophy other than to churn out semi educated people with little imagination. John offered me the position of teacher as soon as we left the dining hall. My job would be to teach the skills needed to live in the big wide world, a place most of the residents would have little experience of, they were just too disabled. St Christophers is a semi residential school in a line of beautiful old mansions, set on the edge of the Downs in Bristol, 10 minutes bike ride from the Avon Gorge and 3 minutes from home. As both of us were teaching we took on a nanny, Tricia, a very religious lady who had worked with the Innuit people in Arctic Canada, she was utterly dependable and had some great stories. Very sadly when she left us she went to Uganda and died of Cerebral Malaria in 4 days. My partner Pippa and I were classroom based some of the time doing money, home, food and garden skills but often we would take groups out to town and visit shops, cafes and supermarkets. One of the great characters was Charlie, a gentle but very scary looking giant, he had a huge jaw and improbably large and pointy teeth, when he got excited he would strangle himself. One day we all went on a boat taxi in Bristol docks, Charlie had clocked that the brass lever told the boat to go forward. As passengers were getting on and off, Charlie reached over and pushed the lever. Pandemonium! The guy holding the mooring rope was being dragged into the dock, passengers were halfway on or halfway off and Charlie was towering over everyone, strangling himself and doing a very loud Charlie version of laughter. I managed to push the lever back before things went totally tits up. All the teachers had to do 1 breakfast shift each week, which meant going in early, help the kids get up, wash and breakfast. I was appointed Fraser, a very Autistic lad. I knew very little about Autism in those days but worked a lot with very Autistic people in the future. Left to his own devises Fraser would have spent the entire day pulling his socks so tight they would rip. I have so much respect for the parents of some of these people, being the parent of a severely Autistic or violent child is a life sentence. I went to the train station at the end of a Summer break to collect Robin, a large but generally peaceable lad. I asked Mum how it went, she said 'Steve, he broke my arm on day 3 and it went downhill from there.' There was some weird financial business going on so I couldn't stay at St Christophers as long as I would have liked, but before I left we had another hilarious afternoon. As all the folk where 19, they had the right to vote, so we invited the 3 major parties to do an election speech. Only the Liberals responded and the candidate duly turned up one afternoon. We were all sitting on sofa's and he started his speech. Charlie was by the door strangling himself, Johny was spinning madly in the center of the room, just the whites of his eye's showing and Julie had her hand down her pants giving herself a good seeing to. After 5 minutes the poor guy goes 'sorry, I just cant do this' and left. Top marks for trying though mate!

I was climbing well at this time, Martin Crocker was 'the man' in the SW and putting up some very hard routes. Martin is tall, I could just reach his clips but many couldn't, I think it amused him. Martin went on to do great services for SW climbing. Cheddar was one of his favourite stomping grounds, and still is. Hard trad routes in Cheddar are testing beasts to say the least, especially onsite, some of the best routes in the country don't get climbed for years. Its the same with Avon, people complain that its loose, funky and scary. Its not. Both places are unique. Its up to you to learn how to climb at these places if that's what you want to do. I clocked up a lot of air miles in Cheddar, hitting the deck from on high on 3 occasions. The last one was particularly memorable. I pulled a massive flake off, hitting the deck from 10 meters then the flake pinned me to the ground. Unfortunately this was seen by a member of the public who dialed 999. The big yellow helicopter picked me up and took me to hospital where they X rayed me till I glowed in the dark and told me 'no one ever survives a fall like that'. I was told exactly the same thing many years later in Australia.

Climbers like to think of themselves as adventurous, 99% of them just want predictable safety. Only a tiny number of climbers get their rocks off by onsiting new routes. That's adventure, and it makes no difference what the grade. Climbing for me has always been about getting from the bottom of a crag to the top just using my hard won skills, my guile and hard won strength, and not leaving a mess behind. Strung out 3 meters above an equalized group of shitty RPs working out the percentages of up, down, will the RPs hold? I usually found that going up was best, the autopilot would kick in and all would be OK. Nipper and I trained hard! We went to a gym once a week, hung round each others waists and did pull ups till we couldn't do any more. Then we went to the pub for 6 pints of Bass.

About this time 2 mates, Steve Berry and Steve Bell started Himalayan Kingdoms, a trekkingcompany and asked me to lead their first trek to Sikkim. Its a very beautiful walk to the Goecha La in the footsteps of Sir Joseph Hooker, an eminent 18th century botanist. My brother John came along and we had a lot of fun!

I was at a bit of a loose end work wise. Angela was ambitious to advance into school management so I agreed I would look after the kids while she got on with her career. Hazel was with us now. I call her Hammy because when she was little her cheeks where so fat you could see her smiling from behind. Hammy the Hamster, she would be my best friend for the next 27 years until she decided to stop talking to me. Angela got a deputy headship in a small special school in Cleveland in NW England. It was not the happiest moment of my life when she came out and announced she had got the job. I knew no one anywhere near there and the climbing looked shit. Actually, its pretty good! I just had to join the local climbing club and get shown around by the locals. We all met in the 'Jet Miner" on a Wednesday evening, told lies and made plans. The local rock was a hard sandstone, very like Grit. As I soon rediscovered, Grit ain't limestone and I was knocked back from hard E6 to about HVS, in fact there is a HVS in Northumberland I never managed to do. It was that first winter at Saltergill I went off with FFFFrancis Ramsay to have a crack at the N Wall on the Eiger. It was so cold! We went straight there and just jumped straight on it, green or what?! Needless to say we ran away. We had a couple more goes together and got spanked each time. I never did much in The Alps, just some good, long rock routes round Chamonix and the Walker Spur in a day in '86.

Back in the NE I met Chris Shorter, who lived just down the road, we did some interesting and hard new routes on the local crags. Chris was a desperate chalky, so every time we went out I would sneak something nasty into his filth bag, stingers, thistles, any kind of shit, rocks, dead rats you name it.

I really enjoyed being a full time Dad! Hammy and I would drop Ben at school, then go do something interesting, we had a great dog, Stubsy, and we all spent a lot of time walking on the North York Moors. When she got tired of walking I would put her on my shoulders, she would fall asleep and flop all over the place. 2 year old's weigh a lot after an hour or so of carrying them in your arms. Sometimes the bracken was so tall I put her on my shoulders so she could 'navigate', over there Dad, that way Dad, random.

After about 3 years Angela got a headship in N Wales in Holywell, we found a beautiful house set in a beautiful large garden. I started a plant nursery to complement my vast collection of orchids. Most people think of orchids as delicate beings, they ain't, they is nails.

They have been around a lot longer than humans and have evolved to live in the harshest of conditions and thrive on every continent other than Antarctica. Like every other living thing on the Planet they have a symbiotic relationship with a micorhirzal fungus. A seed is a single cell and it needs the fungus to germinate. How to grow orchids from seed then? An Agar plate with all the necessary nutrients in a sterile situation does it. I made friends with Bob Dadd, an outright genius who took this science to new levels. One time Kew sent him half a seed capsule containing seeds of Epidendrum ibaguense, an extremely endangered Panamanian species. Kew couldn't get anything to grow, Bob produced thousands of plants and undoubtedly saved the species. He also perfected a way of growing Phalaenopsis plants from the nodes on the flower spikes. He would buy an extremely expensive, awarded plant, often from the USA then produce hundreds of them and sell them to his customers for a fraction of the market price. Orchids fascinated me and I ended up with one of the best small orchid collections in the country. 400+ different species is small by the way. Some wealthy enthusiasts had thousands of orchids and they were all very interesting people! I won a lot of shows for quality growing. Learn, learn, learn!!! I built a large poly tunnel and grew a lot of plants. In the first year I grew 5000 plants from seeds and cuttings, I called the business 'Unusual Perennials' Nipper reckoned that's what I am.

.I   I discovered Gogarth... Positron,Big Groove, Ciitadel and Ordinary route. When Steve Monks and I finished Ordinary we bumped into Paul Pritchard, Noel Crane and George Smith, they asked what it was like? 'Well', I said,'there ain't nothing ordinary about it' I also met the Ormes. Great and Little. I loved the cartoon in the guide book of the time for Little Orme. A tiny figure looking up at the huge crag thinking 'hmm, so this is Little Orme'. When I was climbing on Upper Pen Trwyn my eye was often drawn to a blank piece of rock on Little Orme. I eventually got together with Mel Griffith and produced 'Far away and Long Ago', a 2 pitch 7c that we stapled. I named it so because I knew I was going to have to leave the kids. I had had enough of playing second fiddle to Angela's ambitions, the role reversal had not worked for me. When I said I wanted to go climbing in Jordan she said 'what, on my money? It broke my heart to leave Hammy and Ben.

I had been pissed off for sometime but the catalyst to get me moving was Lisa, a gorgeous little Jewish princess. She was a psychiatric nurse studying at Southampton Uni. She didn't stay there for long, preferring the more practical side of the profession. We set up together back in Bristol, it was great to be back with my old mates again and we soon settled into the routine of having the kids every other weekend. We lived very close to the climbing wall, both Hammy and Ben were very active kids and loved climbing. Hammy of course went on to get quite good, Ben discovered skate boarding, unfortunately this proved to be his downfall in a few years time. They loved to go on adventures. One holiday in Pembroke when there was a big Spring tide we traversed from Chapel Cove right along to St Govans Head exploring the huge caves along the way. I would say 'I bet no kids have ever been here before'! On the way back we climbed out of the descent chimney, Hammy going first, she popped out of the ground right in front of a bunch of tourists, 'where have you come from little girl?' 'Down there', she replied with impeccable logic, then Ben popped out, the onlookers were completely blown away by the time I appeared.

I soon got a 6 month contract working with extremely Autistic kids. The first morning in the staff room, one of the women said 'Steve, do you realise you are not a teacher any more? You are now a zoo keeper', she wasn't far wrong!, 3 staff for 5 kids was barely enough! Luckily the ladies I was working with were very experienced, it was still a very steep learning curve though. I decided the best way forward was to challenge the kids, a philosophy I have always adopted. Too many disabled kids are spoiled, people tend to think 'aw, poor little kids', I had the same expectations of them as I did my kids. Some Autistic kids are very fearful of change and they need a lot of structure. My philosophy catered for this but I would challenge their fears by taking them to places that terrified some of them. Buses, cafes, shops and supermarkets, places the parents wanted to go but were scared to because of the inevitable battle that ensued. The staff were all amazed when I took my group out, but the Head, Steve, the only other man was very supportive of my theories. Every Autistic kid is very much an individual, I referred to their peculiarities as 'flavours'. One lad, James, if left to his own devises would twiddle a straw in front of his eyes for the rest of his life. He screamed and screamed the first few times we went to a supermarket but was fine after a couple of months. These changes for the kids made life so much easier for the families, this was always my main aim. Rhodri would skip about wild eyed, he was a gorgeous little elf with only 1 tooth in his head but still ate his bed, he needed a new one each month. He was an ace escape artist, one day he just disappeared, dozens of people were out looking for him and he was eventually found in the roof above the sports hall! As the end of my 6 month contract approached I applied for a job in another nearby special needs school, Briarwood. I went to see the Head, a really great bloke by the name of Jo Buxton and explained I would like an interview but would be in Kazakhstan on the interview date. He said no problem, we can interview you before you go, then let you know the result. This would involve him telephoning Lisa who would call Jagged Globe, who would Telex Kasbek Valiev in Almaty,who would radio Karkara, they would put a note on a helicopter flying to base camp. Eventually Anatoli Boukreev gave me a note at 5,500 meters on Khan Tengri, it read, 'you got the job, congratulations'.

Briarwood

That Summer was busy! I did the mountain (more later) went home, collected the kids and Lisa, drove to the Ardeche for a 2 week holiday, took the kids home then started at Briarwood the next day. Lindi Reynolds, the Deputy Head berated me for not contacting her, when I explained what I had been up to over the Summer she just looked at me as if I was mad! I was very fortunate to get a job share with Lindy, she was incredibly knowledgeable and a veritable whirlwind of energy. We shared a class of 6 delightful kids. A couple of Downs boys,1 girl who could speak well, Lottie who was just completely mad, Paul, a lovely boy with mild Aspergers and Philip, a very disabled boy in a wheelchair. Philips favourite occupation was masturbating, we couldn't stop him so we would just turn his chair around. I could only get him to do anything by bribing him with cheesy whatsits which he would accept with a beautiful smile. Pottie Lottie would come in every morning unable to see, I would ask her if she had eaten her breakfast with her glasses again and the whole class would crack up. Jo Buxton was a great Head, he would quietly let himself into the classroom and watch, if he thought I could improve on anything he would have a quiet word later. Unfortunately Jo retired.

The next Head was a whole different kettle of fish, he never once came into either of my classrooms. Lindi agreed to stay on for 6 months to help with the change, it was glaringly obvious she wasn't going to get on with the new guy and it was glaringly obvious I wasn't going to either! As soon as he got there he started to implement the National Curriculum, a system obviously invented by some Etonian moron in Whitehall who had probably never even met a disabled kid. We had an inspection coming up, I wanted to show off our garden area but no, I had to do Mondrian art, fucking morons! At the end of my inspection the head of the team asked me if I approved of the National Curriculum. No, I don't! That lesson was the only one I didn't get 100% in. During the first term there a very pretty lady had approached me and said 'you don't remember me do you? When I was 8 your brother tied me to a tree and left me there all day'! It was Sue Martin who lived round the corner from us when we were kids. More of Sue later. I had decided I would like a class of my own, I went in during the Summer holidays with Hammy and painted my new classroom. There was absolutely nothing in there when we started the new term. I was given 5 kids that basically no one knew what to do with, Lindi helped a lot and I had a brilliant classroom assistant.

All the kids were great except 1, try as I might I could not like Scott. Shalainia was gorgeous and very Autistic, it took me months to teach her to be able to step through a doorway. She went from complete inability to taking the class register through 3 doorways to the school secretary and back again, on her own! Her Mum was lovely, she said she would only allow her daughter to stay in the school if I promised her I would not teach her the National Curriculum. I promised. Shalainia had some weird visual / brain problem I never understood and I never worked out if she couldn't talk or wouldn't talk, I suspect the later due to the ever present smirk on her face. Tom had had a 32 hour epileptic fit that had destroyed 80% of his brain, he had to be taught how to eat again, he walked on tippy toes and would never talk again. He was a gorgeous little blue eyed elf and everyone loved him. His Dad was an abusive cunt! Josie was just Josie, she could say yes and that was all. She and her family were all lovely. I started using a system called PECS, picture exchange communication system. I used cheese biscuits as bribery, I took a photo of a biscuit and if the kids gave it to me I would reward them with the real thing. Some could understand the concept pretty quick, some it took months, some like Tom and Scott, never. It proved amazing for some families. A huge problem for many families was the inability of the kids to express what they wanted / needed. I went to the homes of the kids who grasped the concept of exchange and took photo's of the toilet, food, bed, the back door, the car etc and stuck them on a velcro board. When the kids wanted / needed something they could just give Mum or Dad the photo and hey presto. Fucking amazing!!!, and so simple! I got through so many cheese bickies I asked the company if they would like to donate some. They sent a huge box each month, enough to keep the entire school going .

Just one of the amazing ladies at the school was Nina, she ran the PMLD unit, Profound and Multiple Learning Difficulties. Kids who couldn't walk, talk, see or hear. At some stage Nina went off on a sabbatical, I was fascinated by her work but when I had a go I just couldn't do it. Its not that it was sad or anything but there was not enough feedback for me. We had a lot of fun in my classes! I have absolute respect for people like Nina, she had total commitment. She was great in bed too!

Each half term I would choose a different kids book and we would paint the story of the book in fluorescent paint all round the classroom. Every morning we would turn out the lights, turn on the UV and read the story. We even had a UV Owl whizzing across the room, it took ages for the kids to notice it. After about 18 months things started going downhill, I was struggling with having to provide a curriculum neither I nor the parents approved of, it was ridiculous, maths hour, English hour, I was doing battle with the management and I was losing. Badly. Lisa and I had split, Jane went by, Sue split with her man and asked one day if I would like to go for a drink that evening, Yes please! Light the blue touch paper and stand back! One word sums up the next 7 years. Insatiable. I introduced Sue to to clubbing and MDMA, she just loved it! We would go clubbing but after an hour or 2 we would just have to get back to my place, use your imagination! The battle intensified, the next term I was expected to teach my kids equations or something I didn't understand. Fuck it, I was very badly stressed, I went to to the doctor, he told me I was depressed. As I drove home crying, I thought 'the cunts', all I have done for the last 30 years is try to help people' I was in a bad way for some time but Sue was great and we had an amazing time together! I went to Shishapangma, where everyone very nearly died, then I went to Australia.

I decided to steer clear of the 'system'. I started a gardening company, very pleasant, I never made much cash but I didn't need much. I had a lovely little terraced house in Eastville,Bristol, known by all as the garden of Easton. All the tenants who lived there are all still good friends, especially Regan, Ron and Adam. Every Midsummer's Eve I would have a BBQ, crazy, sometimes there would be 50- 60 people in and around a 2 up, 2 down house. I also had the Planets maddest cat, Tash, she hated Chris Savage for some reason,a lovely guy, she just attacked him on sight, every time. Hammy and her climbing friends hung out at no 27, they were all keen climbers, moving on from competitions to the sea cliffs of the SW. Hammy, Ben, her first boyfriend, Jo Stadden and I went to Cornwall for a trip. One day we went to Freedom Zawn, a place I had not been before but it got a good write up. Hammy set off up one route, Ben belayed by Jo set off up another. At about 20 or so feet Ben pulled a hold off and landed flat on his back on a boulder.

Fuck, he's a gonner! Hammy and Jo were beside themselves. Amazingly, Ben seemed OK but I couldn't work out if his back was OK. If he had landed with a cam between him and the rock things would be bad. A tourist called 999 and the coastguard helicopter turned up, while Hammy, Jo and I hid under an overhang the pilot with his rotor tips just inches away from the crag lifted Ben away. Ben's Mum was not well in a hospital in Bristol, I couldn't stop thinking what I would say to her. When we got to the hospital Ben was pronounced OK, Phew! We all went back to the campsite and had a conversation about sea cliff climbing. This was the first time any of them had come across this kind of situation. Climbing is inherently dangerous. I had drilled this into Hammy but its only by experiencing near death situations do you start to understand. I drank a lot of whisky that night !

I got into doing some very loose shit. I always thought I wanted to be good at all aspects of climbing, I wanted to be able to climb anything. There is no shortage of loose rock in the SW but I had only dabbled with it. I had spotted a face on the Culm coast in Devon that intrigued me. I climbed it with Dan Donovan, I reckon in 400 + feet of climbing only about 8 holds didn't fall off. At one point I was on a slowly collapsing pillar of shale playing cards, I collapsed left with it then jumped to the next shale pillar. There was no gear on this pitch, maybe 3 bits of decent gear on the whole route. I called it Blue Bikini because Sue was on the beach wearing a skimpy blue bikini. I was never interested in repeating other peoples XS routes, I looked at Mick Fowlers route Breakaway just down the coast but had no interest in it, I just wanted to find my own stuff. This spell lasted until I reckoned I could climb just about any crap and then didn't bother any more.

Khan Tengri.

The garden business was doing OK and I was guiding some really interesting stuff, Nepal, Bolivia, Argentina, Kenya, Tanzania, Georgia, Kazakhstan, Pakistan, Bhutan, India and Tibet. The garden biz was great in the Summer, not so great in the Winter, I started to go to Thailand in the Winter. More about that later, its where I live now. Two great trips I did were one of the largest and the smallest, Khan Tengri in Kazakhstan and Kasbeck in Georgia. I clocked up about 40 trips in total.

Khan Tengri, (Lord of the Skies) is without doubt one of the Worlds most beautiful mountains. The top 1000 m of its 7000m is white marble, sunsets can be incredible. The first time I went there I was meant to go from the Southern Kirgize side. I took one look and said 'nay'. I renamed the route Death Valley, both sides are enormous avalanche slopes, I got the guys to fly us round to the N side, so much safer! We did the usual acclimatization stuff for a couple of days then should have gone up to C1. I took one look at the mountain at 7 am and informed the clients we would not be going up that day. But the itinerary says....blah blah.. We are not going up! OK? Sure enough at 10 am when we would have been plumb in the middle, the entire face avalanched. You got to listen!!! To what you might ask? I don't know. But you still have to listen. We did the usual, up to C1, back down, up to C1, then C2, then up to C3 and bivy in a snow hole. It was extremely cold! Khan Tengri is the most northerly 7000m peak and it makes quite a difference. The atmosphere thins out rapidly away from the equator, that means the air pressure is lower, its colder and its harder to breath. Its probably about the same as Everest with oxygen. 2 of us made it to the summit, it ain't hard nor is it easy but it is spectacular! I must have been a tad anoxic on the summit, I shoved a screwgate carabiner in my mouth to thaw it out, not a good idea at minus 30!

The gigantic (63k) N Inilcheck glacier sweeps away towards Isikul, the very dangerous Pobeda looms to the South. The Tien Shan is a truly great mountain range. The people who got hard there are truly great also, Anatoli Boukreev, Valery Khrichtchatyi, Kazbek Valiyev , Oleg Malichov to name but a few, all hard as fucking nails and all World class mountaineers. When we got down the guys partied us royally, they were very impressed that I hadn't used guides, this was entirely due to the fact they hadn't told me there were any. Kasbeks base camps were amazing back in the mid 90s, huge military style mess tents, family size sleeping tents, saunas and endless supplies of vodka. The area is seismically very active, one time I was there a mate had just flown in, Oleg had just poured 3 huge vodka's when dozens of also huge avalanches kicked off all down the valley. He waited till things calmed down and then said 'Khan Tengri, she salutes you!' Nastarovia!
When all the guys had flown in that Spring to set up they found that an enormous area, about twenty square kilometers of glacier had dropped by at least 30m, you could still see the marks on the valley walls. It took them weeks to find all the equipment. The last nights all nighter was forever set in stone by meeting Tamara, a truly lovely Kazakh girl. While we were at breakfast and awaiting the helicopter in the morning Aleksy came in and started pouring vodka. I asked, 'Aleksy, do you know the expression 'hair of the dog'? 'Hair of ze dog? 'shit Steve, we shave ze dog'! Oleg gave me my most prized possession, a massive Russian built duvet jacket, sky blue with Kazakhstan embroidered across the back in gold thread. He had spent 4 days at 8,400 meters on Everest with no oxygen and in a storm wearing the jacket. I asked him what that was like? 'Oh Steve' he said, 'it was so boring, all I could do was smoke.'

Georgia

I couldn't help noticing the bullet hole that went through 2 plate glass doors and into the lobby ceiling. As soon as I stepped into the lobby a long line of extremely well armed men came down the stairs. I clocked who was the boss, extended my hand and said 'Hi! I'm Steve, from England'. He replied, 'wow! Steve, from England, do you know George Best'? Within a couple of minutes he was taking photo's of me holding his AK 47. We had been booked into what the lonely planet guide described 'as probably the worst hotel in the Soviet Union'! After I got the clients sorted with their rooms a young couple from Bristol came to my room to tell me that whenever they pulled the flush,raw sewage would gurgle out of the shower drain. I really wish I hadn't checked the kitchen, some dude was in there hacking lumps of meat off the leg of something with a rusty hatchet. The armed guys were stationed at the hotel so they could protect the huge weekly food convoys traveling from Cechneya to Tiblisi. They filled in the remaining time by getting hammered on Cha Cha, loading their AKs with tracer rounds and lighting up the valley. The mountain was cool, a bit over 5000m with a very nice vertical green ice pitch leading to the summit, all the clients rapped down and I dropped the ropes, as I turned round to start climbing down my crampons slipped on the hard ice. I slammed my axe into the ice nearly ripping my arm off but I stopped. Gulp! We returned to Kasbegi. I had requested a bottle of Cha Cha and sure enough there it was waiting on the bar. It was 92% alcohol! After 'dinner' we started on the hooch, one very large guy from Bristol chucked a glass or 2 down, sang 'Drink up thee Zider' twice and didn't move again for 12 hours, others where more cautious. I stayed up late with our excellent guide Valery and we polished it off. The next morning we had to recross the highly militarized pass into Osettia. As we waited in the bus I pointed my camera out the window and a 16 year old pointed his AK at me. Luckily I was called to see the Lieutenant, I walked through cages and cages of weapons and ammunition, the Lieutenant stamped our passports and gave me a memento of Georgia, a live AK round, I got it home in a Titanium ice screw. Next was Elbrus. We had an evening in a rather more salubrious hotel drinking very good Georgian Champagne at $2 a bottle. It was very nice to have a snow machine take us up most of the boring lower slopes early the next morning. Some Russian nutter was doing the mountain dressed only in yellow nylon shorts, it was cold! One of the clients threw a huge frisbee of the top, it just disappeared into the distance and I was invited to join in a game of chess making it probably the highest international game going on anywhere that day. When we flew out of Moscow the immigration guys were really pissed off! 'What is this? There is no such place as Georgia!' When I got back to the office I was asked what I thought of the trip, 'I thought it was great fun'! 'Hmm, that's interesting, the last guide thought it was completely unjustifiable'.

Xtreme Everest

I have never had the slightest interest in climbing Everest. The first time I saw the icefall I absolutely knew it would kill me. Jagged had sent out an email to all the guides asking if anyone would be interested in running a big medical research expedition. That sounded interesting! The research was into how oxygen is transported to individual cells in the body. 200+ volunteers in groups of 10 were tested in Kathmandu, Namche, Pheriche and base camp. Further tests were done in the Western Cwm on the doctors themselves. Volunteers were asked to pedal a bicycle, hard! whilst having their bio metrics recorded on computers. I based myself in Pheriche, a Sherpa village at 4000 meters. I renamed it 'the windy city', every day at 10am the wind would pick up and rattle the town, all day until about 4pm when thankfully it would die down. I stayed with a Sherpa family and it was bloody cold at night, Pemba quickly sorted me with a couple of duvet covers and all was well. The doctors were a seriously clever bunch from all over the World and a lot of them had serious mountaineering experience also. They were equipped with state of the art technology which was carried to BC on Yaks, something that amused me quite a lot. I was in Pheriche for 3 months and was responsible for all the logistics between Lukla and base camp. I had an enormous spreadsheet on the wall in my room and much to my surprise everything went smoothly. I had a small team of Sherpa's, all of them friends from previous trips in Nepal and we all had satellite phones. I have had a strange relationship with sat phones. Before they were regularly issued I never needed one, when we started carrying them regularly I needed one on several life or death occasions. I could never work that one out! Quite a few volunteers wanted to stay on after base camp and go on local side trips like Island Peak or the Cho La. I would give one of the Sherpa's a bunch of cash and say OK, 'see ya in a week'.

The expedition was a big one, it cost about 3 million quid in the end, it was financed by British Oxygen and British Universities. Half a million was donated by John Cordwell, a wealthy British business man. Lydia Bradey and I escorted him up to BC. Lydia was the first woman to climb Everest without oxygen and solo! We hadn't seen each other for about 10 years. We stopped above the Khumbu glacier at one point and John asked what the glacier was all about. I told him the ice was probably 2-300 meters deep and slowly creeping down the valley. 'Where does all the ice come from'? he asked. I told him that the ice comes from avalanches that fall off the sides of the mountains, they could be any size, sometimes millions of tons. He obviously thought I was taking the piss. When we got to BC there was a small reception for him. Just as it started, a truly gigantic avalanche slammed into the glacier only a kilometer or two away. Our eyes met just before the ice cloud enveloped us. He now understood. That one was probably billions of tons!

A Sherpa came tearing into the hotel where a couple of the doctors were staying one evening and told us to 'come quick'! We followed him to another hotel just down the road to find a German girl thrashing around on her bed, she was obviously in a bad way, we bundled her up in a duvet and carried her back. She was a big strong girl, it was a battle for four of us, she was also only wearing very brief white knickers, extremely challenging for Sherpa gentlemen! Gail, the Kiwi doctor radioed the senior doctors at base camp while several of us made sure she didn't hurt herself, the poor girl had no idea what was going on. The doctors decided she had probably got both Meningitis and Cerebral Edema. Not a good combination! A Sherpa started running from BC with intravenous antibiotics while we tried to get some Ketamine into her to calm things down. 4 of us tried to keep her still while Gail attempted to get the needle into her, suddenly the door burst open and a bunch of Sherpa's came in brandishing burning juniper branches and throwing rice everywhere! Gail was shouting 'look, just fuck off will you'!? at the top of her lungs while still trying to get the needle in. It was total chaos! The locals thought she had been possessed by demons! Eventually Gail succeeded and things calmed down a bit, the Sherpa from BC arrived in an astonishing three hours and Gail got the drip going. The girl had to go down asap though. I booked a helicopter for 8 am the next morning, she was still thrashing as we bundled her into the chopper with Gail. Apparently she woke up 3 days later in Kathmandu and asked 'what happened'? She is a very, very lucky girl, to get that sick and have most of the Worlds best high altitude doctors in attendance is astonishingly unlikely!

The only thing you can predict about altitude is that any ailment will always get worse, because someone has been OK once doesn't mean they always will be. I quickly learned that if someone turned up at Heathrow with a respiratory problem I would have to be extra vigilant. One fit young guy turned up with a cold, he had done Aconcagua the previous year. We were in the Rolwaling valley at barely 4000m, quite remote in those days and he got very ill very quickly with pulmonary edema. Amazingly there was another group nearby, even more amazing they had a doctor with them. As she held the stethoscope to his lower back she asked what my plans were. I told her I was planning on sending him down in the morning. She raised an eyebrow and said 'if you wait till morning Steve he will be going down in a box'. Gulp! I immediately set off along with 2 Sherpa's, we only went down a few hundred meters and the guy improved hugely, he continued on down to Kathmandu with 1 of the Sherpa's. When we caught up with him 2 weeks later he was still in a bad way, he would get a taxi down into the city but have to return after a couple of hours completely exhausted. 2 Irish guys turned up with colds and by the time we got to Tagnag at 4000m they were both in a very bad way, again with HAPE. If the weather had been bad and I couldn't get a helicopter they would have both died. The only ways out are 2 days over a high pass or 4 days down the valley.

I had just returned to Kathmandu after a 4 week trip when I was asked to fly back up to replace a guide who had been injured by a falling rock. I flew back up to 5,000m thinking I would be fine as I was well aclimatised, I felt decidedly wobbly and could hardly string a sentence together! I gave Island Peak a miss but went up Lobuje a couple of days later. As I was fixing ropes I had a visual migraine, nothing unusual for me but I felt a flick across my left cheek and another on the back of my right hand. When we got to Namche I called home and talked to Hammy and Sue telling them what had happened. They persuaded me to talk to a doctor in Kathmandu, he sent a helicopter for me. This was a real piss off as I was meant to be meeting 3 mates to do some rather lucrative filming work on Ama Dablam. In Kathmandu I had an MRI scan, the director of the unit greeted me in the corridor and said 'good morning Mr. Findlay, you have sinusitis'. She was one of the smallest women I have ever seen and a Colonel in the Nepali Army. Back in the UK the company insisted I get checked out by Charles Clark, an eminent high altitude doctor and neurologist in Harley street, not a place I was familiar with. He said 'no problem Steve, you had a migraine',he had had a similar event on Everest and lost his sight for 8 hours! I realized I had chosen the wrong career path, Charles charges a minimum of 300 quid an hour, I was getting a measly 70 quid a day for guiding 7-8,000m mountains.

Sue and I split, I don't know why. We where on Lundy and she was just horrible! She often had a hard time when she was away from her kids, but this time.....We both had a very hard time.

I had been spending Winters in Thailand for some time, UK Winters are horrible! Steve Monks suggested I go back to Australia, Good idea!

Australia, deserts and liars.

It was great to be back in Nati, I had spent 3 months there in " 04. I was climbing well then and one of the highlights was The Totem Pole. The 'Tote' would be a great piece of climbing even if it was in some shitty quarry somewhere, its setting on the Tasman peninsula in SE Tasmania is quite stunning! Go do it quick, I cant believe it will be there much longer, the Southern Ocean can generate some huge waves. I climbed a lot at Arapiles and the Grampians but didn't really explore the area. As soon as I got to Nati in 2014 I went to see an old friend, Jane Wilkinson. She and Steve Monks where an item a long time ago and rented a room in our house in Bristol when Ben was very small. Jane came to visit the UK when Ben was 18 and when we were returning from a festival Ben tried it on with her. 'Piss off Ben, I used to change your nappies.' The years had not been kind to Jane but she seemed happy. She had transformed her house from a very average little place to a stunning open, arty place set in a beautiful garden. She also had Sheema, the Worlds funniest dog. We got on very well, we shared common interests, gardening, orchids and nature in general, it wasn't long till I moved in and decided to stay in Australia. It also wasn't long till I realised things were going to be very tedious. Jane slept all afternoon, guzzled beer all evening then staggered off to bed at 9pm. I didn't care, I had discovered Buloke, the Worlds hardest and most beautiful wood. I would spend huge amounts of time creating beautiful things which I would sell at the market and in an art gallery in South Australia. The first friend I made was Sarah, a lovely and very beautiful English girl who lived next door with her partner Tim. We did some great trips with them and other couples to the High Country and S Australia. I was totally captivated by the desert and started reading about the Aborigines. What an amazing people they are!, they truly understand the land they live on and have loved and nurtured for 65,000 years. I urge everyone to read First Footprints by Scott Cane and Kangaroo by Tim Flannery. Soon after I got to Nati I joined the CFA, The Country Fire Authority, an excellent organisation in one of the most fire prone regions anywhere. The first training evening I went to was being led by a guy I knew fairly well, Hilly. He started with a photo of a gigantic forest fire and a tiny fire truck in the foreground. He asked me what I would do if I found myself in this situation, 'I would fuck off home mate'! 'You passed' he said. Hilly is amazing as are so many people in the CFA, his knowledge is encyclopedic, he later taught me to drive the fire truck. One evenings training was particularly terrifying! The trainers lit the nozzle of a huge propane cylinder then showed us how to spread the hose nozzle into a fan and just walk up to it. Ching ching !?

I started going to the desert on my own, the most important thing I ever did. I dont think I ever really learned anything from climbing but the desert taught me a lot! People often asked me what I do in the desert. You don't go to the desert to do anything, you go to the desert to see what it will do for you. I had a Mazda Bravo truck that I gradually did up so it would go anywhere in the desert. Solar powered fridge, dual linked batteries, spare wheels, tools, etc. I discovered the value of dual, linked batteries the first time I went out with the new system. I fell asleep watching Game of Thrones, one episode of G oT equals one battery. If I had not put the connection in I would have been looking at a very long walk! My first solo trip was funny, I went for about a week up the East side of the Flinders Ranges and further North. One evening I was camping in a very remote place watching lights roaming around just above the horizon. I asked the Blackfella's what they were, 'they are Min Min lights', 'what are Min Min lights'? I asked', 'they are Min Min lights'. Non the wiser. When I got back to civilisation, feeling rather proud of myself for having been such a long way, I stopped for a coffee. There was a huge map on the wall, I had barely stepped off the beach! Australia is big! People in Nati kept telling me I was mad doing solo trips out there. Not one single one of them knew anything at all about the desert. The same lot kept telling me I had to have a radio. I got a radio and never got a peep out of it. I took it slow, learning more each trip till I could take on things that had probably not been done before, especially solo. People think the desert is dangerous, to die in the desert you would need to be particularly stupid! Several times I have been way out for a week and not seen anyone. I was interested in a blank area North and West of the Termination Range, so called I guess because that was where John Eyre terminated his search on his first attempt to find the suspected Great Central Sea. I was thinking of crossing the whole region N of Lake Torrens but decided I might be pushing my luck a bit. I went back to Copley and the locals asked where I had been. When I told them they were impressed! They said no one had been out there for decades. I suggested there wasn't much going on out there. 'Nah mate there's fack all'! I did actually find quite a large oasis with Coolabah's and lots of wild life. One of my favourite places is Lake Eyre, the vast salt lake at the lowest point of Oz, I walked across it once, just me, Nati and a camera.

There was plenty of work for me in Nati, mostly of the gardening variety, it was great, $25 an hour, it was always sunny and never very hard, I could just work when I wanted. The first job I got was with Joan, a lovely old lady who's garden had got a bit too much for her. She paid me to garden but we spent just as much time talking and drinking tea. She, like my Mum had swallowed the Western lies about Islam and was most surprised when I told her I had lived in several Muslim communities and had never met a Muslim person I didn't like. She was a member of a peculiar sect, the Lutherans believe that only those who believe in Jesus Christ go to heaven, what happens to the rest of humanity god only knows. I very much enjoyed organising a couple of large charity fund raisers. The first for the Nepal earthquake, the 2nd for Syrian refugees, we raised a lot of cash! My daughter and Alex Honnold gave talks and definitely helped draw the crowds. I loved exploring the Wimmera, a vast area in the NW of Victoria. It is big cereal farming country but with some area's of remarkable beauty. The saltlakes especially. I could never understand why no one else ever went to see them. No one in Natimuk went there. I would show people photo's of Wyn Wyn or Mitre lakes and nobody knew about them and they where just a few Ks down the road! After I was in the CFA for a while whenever there was a call out everyone would ask me where to go, amazing! Such an incredibly boring bunch of people! My desert trips were becoming more and more important to me. After a couple of years I felt pretty competent and had few concerns. I was in touch with Paul Pritchard who lives in Hobart. Paul had had a very bad accident on the Totem Pole 20 years previously which had left him disabled. He and a few other disabled mates where going to cycle from Lake Eyre to Kosiosko. Lowest to highest. They are all a complete bunch of frauds, there's nothing disabled about any of them. I met them near Lake Eyre and spent about 2 weeks with them, it was a lot of fun! It was hard work for them the first few days on corrugated sand but after that a lot cruisier. I would tag along then nip off with Nati to check out some interesting side track. After a week or so we got to Lyndhurst, an ex coal mining town. As we were looking around for a camping place 2 police ladies asked what we were up too. We explained and Tiffany, the Sergeant invited us to stay at her place. When we got settled (I had a bed in my truck of course) I went over for a chat, She was feeding a baby Kangaroo, they were just about as cute as each other. I asked 'so what to you do out here'? 'We feed baby Kangaroos' she said. Ching ching?! Seriously, they pay this lady $75,000 to feed joeys! Lyndhurst is a town of about 500, mostly black fella's, Tiffany never had to do anything in 5 years! When she went to bed I tapped on her door and asked if she would like some company. 'Nah, I'm OK mate'. Rats! We all got down to Parachilna pretty quick the next day, just a 100k. Tiffany was preying on my mind so I drove all the way back to the police station and asked her if I could take her out to dinner. 'Sorry mate, I'm too busy'. Ching fucking ching!? I did hear a few months later that she had a boyfriend. We crossed the Flinders Ranges in a couple of days, took Nati for a helicopter ride then dropped down to the saltbush plains on the East side, an area I knew well. The guys were on tarmac for the rest of their trip so I left hem at the Barrier Highway and headed South. The next couple of days changed my life, again.

I have always known about a Life Dimension. It has enabled me to know if my daughter was hurting even though she was on the other side of the planet, it has saved my life in the Himalayas on many occasions and it has kept me alive for the last 9 weeks when I have not eaten. I have just accepted these situations as normal.
Once, I was returning from a remote desert region in South Australia. I had to cross a nearly 1000k area of Mallee forest called Danggali, no one lives there. I have crossed this area several times and once before at night. This time I realized I was in a place I didn't recognize. I needed to go South, but none of the tangled mass of tiny faint tracks went South, I drove for 5 hours in the dark then at 11pm I decided to stop. When it got light the next morning I found I was exactly where I wanted to be, within a few meters. To put this in context its like driving from Melbourne to Adelaide with your eyes closed and stopping right outside your front door.
I realised this was not reasonable.
I'm a very good thinker but could not make any headway at all, for weeks I struggled with this problem but got nowhere until I went to a local salt lake with a 13 year old girl named Milly. I soon realized that she knew exactly where she was even though she had never

been there before, I have never met anyone else who could do this. I always know exactly where I am, I don't need maps even in the Australian desert.
I was searching for connections, and after a couple of weeks it slowly dawned on me that there was a connection between Hammy, (my daughter) my Danggali trip and Milly's abilities, it was my old friend the Life Dimension.
I quickly reasoned that this dimension has no limits, not in Australia, not on Earth so it must be a Universal dimension. I briefly tinkered with the Aboriginal " Dreamtime" but rejected it as it is largely a Western construct.
The dimension would have the property of allowing life to arise anywhere in the Universe.
The reason the Life Dimension is so powerful in Australia is because the Aboriginal people have nurtured it for at least 65,000 years. the West chose to drown it in lies and corruption. This is why Western industrial society is fucked. The West will die badly at some point but the Aboriginal people will carry on happily on their beloved unpolluted land.
Then I started thinking about where thoughts come from and where thoughts go to and how this may fit in with the First Law of Thermodynamics, thoughts must be energy and therefore they cannot simply disappear. They come from and go to the Life Dimension. Sentient life throughout the Universe "borrows" thought energy and pumps back vast amounts of energy in the form of thought.
This obviously has implications for Religion, actually I think it slips a noose round the neck of religion and also has huge ramifications for our thinking on birth and death.
It will also be of interest to the researchers who are seeking to understand the nature of the energy content of the Universe.

I have sent this piece out to quite a few people, most ignore it as rubbish of course, but a few really smart people, doctors, physicists, thinkers and engineers have said 'why not'? The Universe is not how it appears. Humans have barely scratched the surface of understanding it. The Aborigines would understand, I wish I had had the chance to talk with them.

I had unconsciously stopped eating whilst being out in the desert. A very interesting spin off from this time was that every ailment I ever acquired just disappeared. I broke my lower back on a trampoline when I was 14 and my Coccyx 20 years later jumping into a river in France. I had never had a day without pain, often very bad. When I hit 60 it was so bad I couldn't walk in the mornings. I went for a CT scan, the doctor looked at it and said 'yer fucked mate'. I had a large Bakers cyst behind my right knee which the medics said would never go without surgery. It went, varicose veins, even athletes foot, gone, and 18 months later, still gone. I still only eat very small amounts of food.

Soon after I got back to Nati Sarah came back from a trip to the UK, I walked the 500m to her house to say hi, she gave me a kiss and a hug and lay back down on the floor, she was obviously trashed so I only stayed long enough to say Hi to Milly, Sarah s foster girl. As I left the house I realised I had fallen head over heals in love with Sarah! Shock set in! I thought about it for a day then found a pearl and sapphire ring my Mum had given me a long time ago. I went round to talk to Sarah but only Milly was there. Milly had had a tough child hood, but we got on really well. I think I was one of the few men she liked and trusted. She liked to cook for me, I think I amused her. I asked if she fancied going out for a drive with Nati and I. 'Yeah, OK'. We went to Wyn Wyn salt lake and I got her to have a go at driving my truck, very funny! I asked if she knew where Sarah's house was and without even looking up she pointed in the right direction. Very interesting! I drove further round the lake and found the tiny faint track we had come in on. 'How did you do that'? she asked. I just said 'I always know where I am'. She looked at me oddly. Milly, although blue eyed and blonde haired has a fair amount of Aborigine in her make up. When we got back to my place Milly said she had to go meet a friend, I put the ring in her hand and said 'give this to Sarah please, its important'. It was symbolic for me, it was saying that Sarah and Milly were an item. Sarah and Tim had split because she wanted kids and Tim didn't. They were very much in love and Sarah was heart broken, I'm sure Tim was too but he's an Aussie bloke. Sarah had met a few guys but none had rung her bell. A few months before I text her one day, 'I think I should get you pregnant Sarah! She replied 'if I'm not sorted by age 37 I will bear that in mind, thanks Steve'. I didn't see her the next day but the day after we where both at a community meeting. She gave a smile that said everything, it was the most beautiful thing I had ever seen. She came over at the end of the meeting and said 'we should talk, I will come round tomorrow' She did. 'Steve, the ring is Hammy's I cant take it', 'keep it Sarah and think about it'. We already had plans to go to Greenland and Nepal together, as friends. I offered to pay for Milly to come as well. She was all smiles and danced her way out of my garden. I heard nothing for a couple of days, (she 's a very busy lady) then I invited her over for curry and a chat, unfortunately, I broke down out in the Desert and was late back. A few more days later she gave me the ring back in the most horrible way. If all things had been equal Sarah would have come to see me, given me a big hug and said 'thanks Steve, but'... Then she would have checked to see if I was OK every day. I knew something was very wrong but had no idea what. The story of the next 6 months is one of pure evil and I do not use that word lightly.

I had left Jane 9 months before when I couldn't take the drunken rages any more. I went next door and asked Jessie if a could rent their empty house across town. She was holding a beautiful black and white pup in her hands. The legendary Nati, the most beautiful, smartest; happiest, most loyal dog ever.

I knew Wilkinson had been lying about me since the day I left, several people had told me. Our best friends, the Eubergangs had promised to look after us equally, they never darkened my door again. I didn't care, I had long known they where weak little people. 1, a member of a sect that believed only he and his droogs would be going to heaven, sod the rest of humanity, the other a fully paid up member of the organisation that has killed, raped, maimed and tortured more than any other, the catholic church. Things where fine at first, I was helping a mate create a new garden and still exploring the Wimmera, but then I started to hear whispers about me being a drug user and having drug induced mental health problems and it seemed people believed them. Peter Mellington, the local policeman and the CFA Welfare Officer came to see if I was OK, I was at the time, then people started avoiding me, they walked past me in the street. I had spent weeks and hundreds of dollars in diesel making a slide show on the Wimmera for the Nati Frinj arts festival. I was the only person not to be invited to the post Frinj dinner. I never heard from any of my many Wimmera bee keeping friends again. To cut a long story a bit shorter, when Wilkinson heard that I had proposed to Sarah she told the Eubergangs who were good friends with Sarah that I was an alcoholic, a drug abuser and that I had drug induced mental health problems. Sarah believed them along with everyone else. If I heard a friend was in such trouble I would immediately offer help.

During the entire 6 month debacle not 1 single person in Natimuk ever asked if I was OK. So much for the caring community eh Jessie ?

Obviously, having 2 people you love ripped out of your life by lying bastards and being shunned is going to have consequences. When I realised how depressed I had got I called the CFA welfare people. The Chaplain came to see me the next day and we had a good chat, he couldn't do much of course but agreed it was an evil situation. I took out an injunction to try and stop the lies but they just carried on. The local police officer took an interest, for some reason I never quite understood he wanted me to see the mental health team and get checked out in hospital. We had a very funny afternoon in the hospital, at one point he accused me of smoking a lot of weed but quickly backed down when I jumped down his throat. I was pronounced remarkably healthy with not a trace of drugs in my system.
One very hot day I was feeling particularly low but Nati and I went out for our daily wander, this time towards a very dry Natimuk Lake. We sat under a tree for some shade and poof!! all the gloom and depression just vanished. Instantly! I don't understand either. We continued our walk and ended up near Sarah's house and called in for drink from the garden tap. While we were there Milly turned up on the school bus. Normally whenever I had seen her around town I was greeted with a big smile and a 'Hi Steve'! Not this time, she turned white, jumped on her bike and pedalled away as fast as she could! I had learned a thing or 2 in my 30 years working with abused kids. I immediately realised that Milly had been told to be afraid of me, someone had told her I would abuse her.
  When I was teaching I had been falsely accused of abusing a child in my class, there was a Department of Education enquiry and I was cleared. Wilkinson was the only person in Australia to know

this story, she told the Eubergangs, oops! she forgot the being cleared bit, and they, for some vile reason told Milly. I conferred with 2 doctors and 2 lawyers then went to the police. It took a little while to go through the system then the hate levels went into orbit! Pat Ford, my best mate had told me that he had moved his family out of Natimuk 20 years previously because they couldn't cope with the Eubergangs lying and meddling. He congratulated me on maintaining my integrity then dumped me in favour of the liars.
 The oh so clever people of Natimuk were too dim to realise you don't get to be a permanent resident of Australia with child abuse on your record, and so incredibly stupid they couldn't work out that maybe, just maybe the Victoria Police would have done a bit of checking. The first thing they would have done is contact the Department of Education in London to check my story. Duurr!, so obvious!
I didn't care, I was going to Thailand. I had decided to go there, find me a girl then move to Tasmania or S Australia. I parked my truck in Monks back garden, a place I had spent a lot of time caring for whenever they were away. I had asked Monks on at least 4 occasions to intervene with the cunts driving me out. He let me down every time. As Joan said, 'that small man.' As far as I know, my gear is still there, festering in his garden. Just before I left I heard that Wilkinson was still telling people that I had left her for Sarah. I sent her a note when I got to Thailand playing on her anxieties, it was pure, cold vengeance for the incredible damage she had caused to so many friendships. I didn't lose any friends of course but a lot of people lost me as a good friend.

                                  Thailand, part 1

The first things 2 things I did when I landed on Phuket were to find a nice little room right by the sea and buy a boat which I moored at the Marina just round the corner. When I went for coffee at the Marina I soon got chatting with Nong, one of the waitresses. She kept asking if she could clean my boat to earn a few extra Baht, but didn't quite grasp the fact that I was the proud owner of a 4 meter inflatable, not one of the enormous floating mansions out in the bay. She told me she worked 12 hours a day, 365 days of the year and took home about $300 a month. She was allowed to sit down for 10 minutes a day. She had 2 ancient parents, an 18 month old son, a sister and brother, they were very poor. This was the first of many many lessons in how tough things are for so many Thai women. We arranged for me to take her for a spin in the boat the next morning but she didn't show, her mate told me she would not be in that day. The following day she said her brother had been involved in a motorbike accident. The next day she told me the true extent of his injuries. He had been knocked off his bike by a hit and run driver, so no insurance. Both his legs were broken, he had lost an eye and an ear, he had also lost his speech. The family were obviously in big trouble, they couldn't get anywhere near paying the bills, she asked if I could help. I told Nong to pack in her shitty job, I would take care of things. As soon as the family had sorted things out I set off for Ko Yao Noi, (Little Long Island) an island about 15 k East of Phuket that I had been to many times to climb. As soon as I got out of the marina I realised I was in for a tough day. I had never seen the Andaman sea so rough! A horrible 1 meter + chop coming from all directions, I had go slow and jam myself across the back of the boat. Basically I got beat up for 8 hours and arrived in the dark. I spent a few days sorting things and enjoying the place, I had forgotten how much I love Thailand, then I set off for Ao Nang to find me a girl. It took just an instant.

                                                Aoy (Sugarcane)

To leave Paradise and someone who loves you beyond reason and return to a situation you hate is the best definition of insanity I have come across so far.

The Issan girls are one of the finest groups of people I have ever met. I always describe them as a, gorgeous b, hard as nails and c, extremely clever. I wonder now if I should add a d, very sad.

My wife Tan told me recently that she had never been happy before, I think that is quite a statement for a 42 year old woman to make and it got me thinking.

I met Aoy at 8pm on the 8th of May, exactly 1 year to the minute since she started working in the bar. She was dazzling! All teeth and glittering eyes. And that smile! We fell in love instantly.
 I picked her up at the pier on KYN the next day, all her worldly possessions packed into a small suitcase. She immediately fell in love with my little Muslim island, its peace and calm and tranquillity. I was making a book of photographs of the island at the time, as soon as she picked up my camera I realized she had talent. She immediately knew what makes a good photograph. She came to my house, a small bungalow set in beautiful gardens, rice paddy and Mangrove. She thought she had died and gone to heaven. As her story unfolded I began to understand why. Born into a large poor rice farming family of 9 in Issan she had a happy childhood, but when school ended at 17 she moved to Udon Thani and started work in an electronics factory, 10 hours a day, 6 days a week, $8 a day, any spare cash she sent home. She lived in a small concrete box near

the factory. She was unhappily married for 8 years and when she left she unusually left the kids with Dad, its usually Gran who looks after them. For some reason she moved to Bangkok and did another 10 years, 6 days a week, 2 weeks a year off to go see Mum and the kids. She had a boyfriend for 5 months during this time but said she spent most of that time trying to get rid of him.

I had decided to have my bothersome teeth removed and have dentures fitted. After 2 excruciating hours having them ripped out of my head I had my gleaming white choppers fitted. I went downstairs and smiled at Aoy, she glanced up from her phone and said 'but I like you with no teesh' I reckoned she had enough teesh for both us and anyway who needs teesh in Thailand? I never bothered with the dentures. She was the funniest person I have ever met, she would stand up on the bar rail, punch em out and have everyone in the bar mesmerised by her 5ft nothing of pure comedy power. She spoke 7 languages.

One evening she started telling me about her life in the bar, she said that some of the girls where OK with the work. Aoy was not! She hated it! She couldn't go with a man unless she was drunk, 5-6 shots of Sangsom would do the trick and she always needed jel. She cried her little heart out as she told me. The first month she stayed with me she slept 14 hours a day, sleeping off the horrors of the previous 20 years.

She also told me a lot about the way the bar worked, basically it was the cash generator that supported thousands of families all across Issan. The owner, Amy, a charismatic and gorgeous woman who used to be a man, like all the girls worked 7 nights a week, 50 weeks per year. Any of the girls, all from Issan, or any of their families could ask for help at any time. She always had between 20 and 30 girls working there and they all extracted as much cash as possible from the customers in the most charming manner. Aoy would start work at 8pm and finish anywhere between 2am and 6am when she would return to the little concrete box she shared with her only friend, Bee.

The main aim of all the girls was to meet a 'farang' a white guy who would take care of them in Thailand or elsewhere. Its one of the few ways out for an Issan girl. Many men would return to Issan with their new girl, there they would spend savings and pensions building houses, raising kids and educating children. So, a bar in S Thailand keeps thousands of families going all across Issan, pumps serious amounts of cash into the poorest province of the Kingdom and sprinkles Issan girls all over the globe.

We continued our idyllic lifestyle, taking photo's, fishing from my boat, dining out in excellent local restaurants and going to our favourite bar a couple of times a week. Life was good! Then one day after 5 months she just disappeared. We were at a small gathering in our usual loved up state, she got up to talk to someone and I never saw her again. Many months later someone told me she had been seen running around shouting bad stuff, Aoy didn't do 'bad stuff'. When I got home she had packed up her stuff and gone.

I was shocked to the core! but decided it was her choice and I would wait for her. I wasn't going to sit at home being miserable though. I got on the excellent Thaifriendly website and made appointments with women all over Thailand. They were all lovely, all beautiful, all single Mums, all broke and all looking for a man. They took me to some amazing places, temples and religious works of art.

About 2 weeks after Aoy left I was at home one morning and had 'one of those moments,' I knew things had changed for her, sure enough, a few minutes later she text me, 'I OK now'. I begged her to come home but she said 'I cannot come home to you, I not perfect for you'. She had judged herself and found herself wanting. A few days later she text me at 3.30am ' I just finish work', she was back in the bar.

Outwardly, I was fine, I was meeting some really great ladies. They were all from the same mold as Aoy and Tan, miserable years in factories. One particularly lovely and gorgeous girl was Nong. She worked in a massage parlour on Phuket, she earned hardly anything, was bored stupid, but mostly she was homesick. She had 2 small girls and 2 old parents. I gave her enough cash to go home and train as a beautician. I went to visit, the family lives in a large shed in a rubber plantation and were very happy. Tan and I still help the family.

Sara also stands out! Way beyond ravishing!! gorgeous doesn't get anywhere near it! She had a small beauty shop that she rented out for 9000 baht a month, her room rent was 7,500 a month. She had a 10 year old boy and two ancient parents in the far East of Issan. She and a small group of girls ran a rather classy little escort agency in Patong, a couple of dudes a month and the girls could feed the family and pay the rent. Sara was happy with what she did.

Inwardly I was sliding into a deep depression but 'luckily' I had met Tan. The second time I went to stay with her and her lovely family I told her about Aoy and completely fell apart. She just held me and promised she would never leave me and would always take care of me. The next day Tans son was being ordained as a monk in the local temple. I was invited to attend, the first outsider ever to do so. As I sat quietly listening to the prayers I felt much of the pain and anguish radiate away. When I stepped outside I was nearly my normal self again. The family where so happy. The next day Tan woke me at 9am and informed me we were getting married, ching ching!? 'when?' I asked, 'now' she replied, ching ching!? We went next door to see Great Great Grandma who tied a white string round our right wrist and said Prayers, then everyone else did the same. Then we drove the short distance to Issan were Tans natural Dad (a Hindu Holy man) tied a much thicker string around our left wrists. The deed was done, we were man and wife.

Tan is one of those really annoying women, with Aoy, Nong, Sara, Nim Nim, Mee Mee, Pla, Aya ,Joy, Jane, May, I could just vaguely point my camera in their direction and come up with a beautiful portrait, Tan, (who everyone else calls Thai, don't ask me why) is desperately difficult to accurately depict.

I was starting to work out what happened with Aoy. I remembered once I had asked how she ended up in Ao Nang, 'I don't know' she said in a sad little voice, what happened to all the cash you earned in the bar, 'I don't know'. (Girls can earn at least ten times as much as in a factory) Before Ao Nang she told me she she had cut off her meter long hair and lived in a temple for 5 months, 'why you do that Na lak'? (lovely), 'I don't know'. The last text she sent me read 'please don't tell me if you have a good time, I hope you understand.' I do now Na lak.

I thought I would never get over Aoy but 10 months later I have. She is still one of the most astonishing and loveliest people I have ever met. She wouldn't come back to me because she loves me so much. She sentenced herself to years and years of doing something she hates because she believed I could do better. She was right, after being with Tan for 8 months I say 'kapum kup' Aoy. I heard recently she has an English boyfriend, I hope she can stay with him. She's an Issan girl and the best advise I can give any man is to spend some time with an Issan girl. Na lak, mak mak !!!

I tried hard to get this published, I don't know how many emails I sent out, it saddens me, and really pisses me off that no female editors picked up on it. I dare you to imagine a more female story and it raises so many issues.

Thailand Part 2.

The first time I went to Thailand was very nearly my last. Sue had been to Ton Sai the previous year and really enjoyed it. A group of 15 or so of us, all climbers went out for a 2 week holiday. We had a couple of days sightseeing in Bangkok then headed for Ton Sai, Asia's premier climbing venue. 6 of us got up early to go do a climb on Ao Nang tower, a 3 pitch 7a. I was climbing with Ben West, Hammy's first boyfriend, we nipped up the route, clipped a 70m line into the anchor and rapped into the boat. No sooner had we done this than the sea started ripping past the tower, stirring up silt. Whats going on asked Ben. 'Bloody good question mate but I know the tide doesn't do this anywhere in the World'. Ben, the boatman and l turned round and all went 'fuck'! A couple of Ks out a huge wave was heading our way, slowly breaking from the right, I suggested to our boatman we try and get out over the wave but we soon saw another longtail try the same thing, it flipped over backwards, I would be very surprised if anyone survived. We turned and went behind the tower into a bay surrounded by small crags, by the time we turned to face the wave we where sitting on the bottom. 2 guys in a boat nearby were chucking bags of rice out, I didn't see them or their boat again. The tower split the wave, 2 enormous churning masses of brown water slammed into us. I vaguely remember being thrown through the air and being brutally washing machined. The anchor line was twisted round my ankle, I couldn't get to the surface, the lights were going out when I managed to get a gulp of air and a glimpse of Ben diving towards me. I managed to untangle myself and get to the upturned boat myself. It turned out that our life long boatman couldn't swim, a ratsucky bit of life jacket turned up and we tied it round him just before the next huge wave arrived. This one was proper wave shaped, Ben asked 'what do we do'? Ben's a surfer and I was no stranger to the sea so we dived into the bottom of it as you usually do, trouble is, there ain't no other side to a Tsunami wave, again we were washing machined along the bottom, I have no idea how far down we were! Again we all surfaced, this time much further back into the bay. The boat was completely fucked! I thought it was time we got to know our boatman, Ben and I swam round and shook his hand, 'I Hassan' he said. A few small waves went through so we headed for the back of the bay, we stood looking at the wreckage. Hassan just kept saying 'my boat, my boat', I even found my rucsac but no camera, shame, as I had great photo's of the wave. We had to run back into the jungle to escape from a 3rd huge wave. We thought the girls were in Ao Nang so we headed that way, there wasn't anywhere else to go really. As we walked towards a building site Ben turned to Hassan and asked 'So, does this happen often around here then? Hassan looked horrified as he told Ben, No! Never! The new development was trashed! Buildings flattened, machinery thrown around, on the far side a delivery ship maybe 40m long had been picked up and thrown into the jungle. Ao Nang didn't look too bad, it has quite a high sea wall protecting it, just a few walls and windows had been punched in. We said our goodbyes to Hassan then walked round town for hours and hours, asking, asking, but no news. Eventually we met the other guys who had been rescued off the tower by the police and we agreed it was best to head back to Ton Sai. Ao Nang was chaotic with rumors of more big waves, thousands of people were heading for Krabi airport. Ben and I watched guys in budgie smugglers sprinting up the street, suitcase in hand. We took the rough path back over the hill and down to Ton Sai. Everyone was in some state of shock, disbelief, no understanding. I don't remember thinking at any stage, hmm, 'so this is a Tsunami'. As people in shock often do we just followed our normal pattern of life, we had a beer, went to dinner and then at about 8 pm Hammy, Sue and the other girls turned up, what can I say? They had persuaded the owner of one of the few boats not to be trashed to bring them to Ton Sai. Phone lines were clogged so we turned to the TV next door. Chaos. It was only over the next few days that the enormity of the situation became clear. I don't remember much climbing being done, we helped out some and tried to have our holiday. One very funny bit was round at Railay beach. There is a shrine in a cave on the beach, thousands of wooden penises of all sizes had been washed away and spread all the way down the beach, the teenage girls in our group were most amused! The rather posh resort of Railay was a complete mess with longtails speared through buildings everywhere. The Ao Nang locals were great, they cooked up various curries and handed them out along with water and beer. I think the Buddhist calm and shit happens attitude is one of the reasons I fell in love with Thailand. After 2 weeks everyone had to go home for work or school, I went to pay the bill. I was expecting it to be rather hefty, 6 of us had hardly stinted ourselves. I was more than surprised when Matt, the boss said, 'Steve, you will never, ever give me any money'. Turned out Hassan was his Uncle. Family is everything in Thailand.

Trevor Massiah, Babs and Kiera came out. Trev had been going to Thailand for ages and put up loads of new bolt routes. I've had many conversations with younger people about how sport routes get there. None of them have the slightest clue. When I tell them old gits like me, climb a crag, on gear, rap down and bolt it they are wide eyed with amazement! The adventurous young couples of Europe and the USA actually have to think! Shock, horror!!. Onsiting new routes in Thailand is challenging and sometimes very dangerous. Very few people have onsited new routes on Thai rock. I did quite a few including some limestone towers behind Ao Nang. We would leave a coin on the summit with the Kings head looking out over his Kingdom. I had just finished leading a rather nasty and dangerous new pitch in the Hollow Mountain when I was struck by lightening! A mate nearby said I turned bright blue for an instant!

Trev knew some guys who knew about an island 100 k or so South of Ao Nang. It sounded like paradise and it is. Laoliang. I made a beautiful little film with Marcus Taylor about the bird nest collectors on Laoliang. "The Bamboo Climbers", you can see it on Youtube. I went to Laoliang for many years until Micha turned up, a gorgeous green eyed German girl who could climb! She said 'come with me to Ko Yao Noi.' Micha and I had a very fine time together!

Meesh and I went to Mianmar on our Honda Waves, as you do. On the way back we stopped in at a village near Ao Luk and just down the road we found a Tsunami museum. I told my story as the curator showed us around. Meesh and I stopped in front of a photo we recognised as the place we had been just 10 minutes before. It looked like a fleet of bulldozers had been over the area. The curator told us that just 2 people out of 1500 had survived, one guy had been fishing out at sea and not noticed when the waves passed under his boat. When he got home there was nothing left.

Tans Dream

Ko Yao Noi is now my home. When I first arrived here I realised how gorgeous the place is and soon learned how lovely the people are. When I was here before (I was in Oz for nearly 5 years) I was a bit insulated from the real KYN, I was climbing and not really getting to know the inhabitants. Now I have learned what a lovely bunch they are. The complete opposite to the sycophantic cowards in Natimuk. I had put in a great deal of time with Aoy and all my cash into producing a seriously beautiful book of photographs of the island. I would make money. Wrong! It turned out that island hopping tourists don't want to lug a 1.5 kilo book around, I lost everything. When Tan and I got together we had fuck all and it was scary but we agreed it was a great way to start a marriage. I know! My mates will help. Wrong! I sent out an email telling my mates 'I need help'. I said I had given quite a lot of cash to Nongs family and the book project wasn't working out. I sent maybe 40 emails out, 6 people replied. 3 friends were happy to help, they are for sure the least wealthy. Kapum kup Ruth, James and Amy.1 of my oldest friends replied 'I will ask around, see if anyone is interested' She lives in a multi million pound house in one of the wealthiest parts of the UK.

 2 others replied with outright hostility.

The 2 people I had worked the hardest for, for so many years. The 2 people I had put myself in harms way for. The 2 people I had worked for free of charge so they could get their business going. The 2 people who had depended absolutely on my honesty and integrity on so many occasions. The 2 people who had got rich from the services of people like me. The 2 people who's asses I had hauled out of the flames so many times. The 2 people who now wouldn't spare me the price of an evening out or even a kind word, Steve Bell and Steve Berry. The shear viscous arrogance displayed by the both of them was nothing short of astonishing! Berry thought I should claw back the money from the families. Bell refused to help me sell my truck and boat then spread vile lies about me to all my friends in Nepal and the UK.

 I didn't lose any friends of course, but a lot of people lost a good friend in me. If any one one of those people had written to me saying 'I need some help' I would have bunged them $100 without even thinking about it, cunts !

Tan and I were in trouble, we could survive, but only just. I really needed to sell my paddle board business. I asked round the island and Phuket, everyone was struggling, it seems Vietnam and Cambodia are so much cheaper than Thailand nowadays, I just couldn't sell them. One morning Tan went to the market, bought a hundred eggs and gave them away to friends, I sold all the boards that day. Tan is a very wise and spiritual lady, she has an unshakable faith in the power of Prayer. I have never given Prayer much thought, but something was looking out for us. I have complete faith in the Life Dimension and Karma. We would survive but it was hard to see how we could flourish and help others. Mum came to the rescue, she had been far too sick and far too sad for far too long. She dropped off the perch at exactly the right moment. Kapum kup Mum, mak mak!!

Tan and I have opened a shop on Ko Yao Noi selling alcoholic ice cream, coffee and cake. Tan has had a very, very hard life!, we called the shop Tans Dream.